MILFORD

Lost & Found

By the Author of

An Historical Account of Charles Island

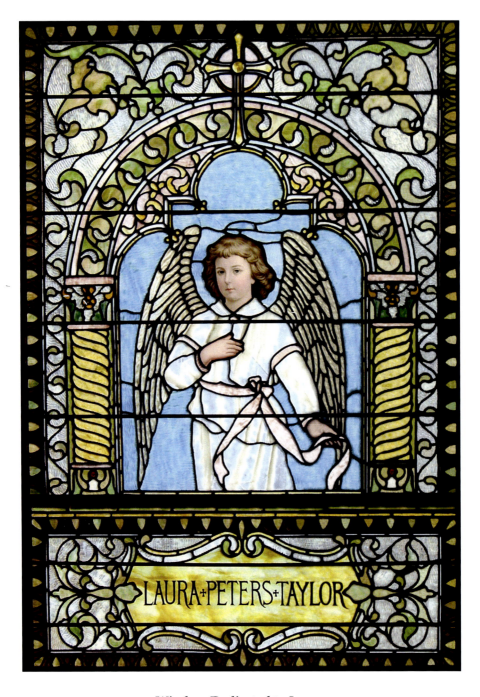

Window Dedicated to Laura
Courtesy of the Mary Taylor Memorial United Methodist Church

MILFORD

Lost & Found

MICHAEL C. DOOLING

THE CARROLLTON PRESS

MMIX

© 2009
Michael Carroll Dooling
Rare Books & Manuscripts, LLC
Middlebury, Connecticut

First Edition

ISBN # 978-0-9627424-2-2

No part of this book may be reproduced or utilized in any form or by any means, digital, electronic or mechanical without permission in writing from the author and publisher.

Printed in the United States of America by InstantPublisher.com

MILFORD *Lost & Found*

Contents

	Page
Introduction	6
Foreword	7
Useful Knowledge and Piety	9
Connecticut's Sleepy Hollow	15
Past Tents on Welch's Point	22
Milford 31, Bulldogs 0	32
For the Love of Laura	39
Sahara Sands on Smith's Point	49
The Tragic Pajama Parade	53
Thoroughly Modern Milford	59
The Greatest Amusement Sensation	63
Milford's Own Father Flanagan	70
Close Shaves for Milford	82
References	90
Notes	92

Introduction

History is made up of many small stories, mostly local and personal in nature. It is these many smaller stories that together make up the sweep and drama of the history we learn in school. But the local and personal can be lost in these general histories.

Michael Dooling has done Milford a great favor in first bringing us his *Historical Account of Charles Island*. This proved to be far more popular here than he expected. He now has presented us with some fascinating stories and many, if not most of them, were unknown to us. While I was familiar in a general way with some of the stories there were others I hadn't heard of at all. I thank Mr. Dooling for bringing to me much that I did not know.

As with his Charles Island book, Mr. Dooling's research has been thorough and exhaustive, and his writing style brings the stories to life. I invite Milford people to sit back and enjoy these little-known vignettes from our past.

Richard N. Platt, Jr.
Milford City Historian

MILFORD *Lost & Found*

Foreword

The collective memory of any community is frighteningly short. Events happen, sometimes history is made, and people remember for a while. Major occurrences become firmly entrenched in the community at large and those stories are passed down to the next generation and documented by historians. Others, perhaps less impactful, are gradually forgotten as memories fade. These bits of history become "lost" in a sense. At the time they happened they added color to people's lives, were discussed at the dinner table, and in various ways influenced the community.

In their time, many of the topics included in the present work didn't seem to be anything more than the stuff of daily living. Who would have thought that a 19th century nickname for Milford might have its roots in American literature, that a group of kids camping on a beach would have any historical significance, or that a company of pioneer filmmakers might make their mark in Milford. Historic events are happening all around us but we don't think of them as such. History is viewed as something ancient, not recent. But it doesn't take long for recent to become historic. Which events of today will be remembered and which will be lost in history's dustbin?

Many organizations and individuals helped this project along the way. I want to thank Municipal Historian Richard N. Platt; Milford's Historical Society, Public Library, Police Department, Chamber of Commerce, Probate Court and City Clerk's office; Connecticut Historical Society, iCONN.org, Connecticut State Library, Yale University Archives, Dartmouth College Library, Smithsonian American Art Museum, Paula Krimsky of The Gunnery Archives, Attorney Robert L. Berchem, the staff of the Academy of Our Lady of Mercy - Lauralton Hall, Sisters of Mercy archivist Sister Dorothy Liptak, Chris Carroll and Richard Sykes of Boys & Girls Village, Bridgeport Public Library, Burvée Franz, DeForest W. Smith, Joseph Finn, Thomas Hilmer, Janet Maher, Rev. Virginia Hoch and the staff of Mary Taylor Memorial United Methodist Church, Ralph & Joy Carloni and family, and to the Gillette Company and BIC Corporation for the generous assistance I received from their Public Relations and Legal departments.

I especially want to thank my wife Joan for her editorial suggestions, support and seemingly endless patience.

View of Milford's Congregational Churches
First Church is on left; Second Church is on right

Useful Knowledge and Piety

Libraries and churches went hand-in-hand in the early Connecticut settlements. Many churches, led by some of the most educated members of the communities, possessed accumulations of books that they would lend to other members of the community. Milford's first two libraries were founded in such a manner. In 1745, the First Church loaned books in its collection to members of their community who could afford to pay ten pounds as a security deposit. The collection was comprised of religious sermons, theological treatises, books on history, travel, and philosophy. With so few works available they were considered highly important to the community, hence the church imposed the required bond.

The Second Church, also known as the Plymouth Church, was founded when a group of parishioners split off from the First Church. The Plymouth Meeting House was built in 1743 but didn't have a full-time minister for several years. In 1747, Rev. Job Prudden, a descendant of Rev. Peter Prudden, became the preacher. He graduated from Yale College in 1743 and was ordained in New Brunswick, New Jersey. Prudden stayed in that position until he died of smallpox in 1774.

During his tenure, Rev. Prudden and members of his parish established Milford's second library - the Associate Library. The original handwritten charter and by-laws, *"made and concluded at Milford this 31st Day of March Anno Domini 1761,"* still exist and provide insight into this early library. The charter consists of 22 articles of agreement and is signed by 127 members of the Second Church.

Detail from Milford Associate Library Charter
The Connecticut Historical Society, Hartford, Connecticut

The new library was founded *"with a desire and view to promote Useful Knowledge and Piety"* and the members agreed *"to unite and join together in a Society...for that purpose; and for that end do agree to have a Library of Books... for the Common Use and Improvement of the said Company, to be known by the name of the Associate Library in Milford."* Members of the library, known as Proprietors, were required to pay dues consisting of *"twenty shillings lawful money"* within one month of signing the charter, the funds to be used for the purchase of books.

The organizers laid out rules regarding the types of books allowed in the library. A committee of learned men was formed to *"chuse the books of which said Library is to Consist."* The committee included Rev. Peter Prudden, Rev. Naphtali Daggett (Professor of Divinity at Yale College), and Rev. Thomas Clap (President of Yale College). One guideline ensured the books were consistent with the church teachings. *"No Book of Divinity shall ever be admitted into said library but such as are agreeable to the Great Gospel Doctrins..."* Another eliminated certain categories of books altogether:

> **No Plays shall ever be admitted into said Library nor any Novels or Romances, which have a tendency to corrupt the Morals of People.**

The library was open but one day per month. *"The second Monday of every other month shall be the fixed times for takeing out & returning in the books & be known by the name of Library Day...and the Library Keeper shall not deliver out any book at any other time."*

In addition to the book acquisition committee the organization had other active members including a Clerk who kept records of decisions and activities. The Treasurer was responsible for collecting monies from Proprietors including dues, donations and fines, and for keeping an accounting of all transactions. A separate committee of five proprietors was responsible for making purchases and assessing damage done to the library's books. Proprietors who didn't pay the assessed fine, *"shall be holly denyed the use of said Library, untill the same be paid."*

The Library Keeper was responsible for the operation of the Library itself and *"shall receive and carefully keep all books...& in each book inscribe the price thereof & that it belongs to said Library & keep a cattalogue thereof...the Library Keeper shall also due information make, of any uncommon damage don to any book, to the aforesaid committee..."* Other articles in the charter addressed problems faced by librarians to this day:

Late Book Fines
Every book shall be returned into the Library on the day fixed & appointed for that purpose...but he that takes a folio or quarto & hath not finished the perusal thereof, before said time of returning it, shall have liberty to take it out a second time if he desires it & whoever shall detain a book unnecessarily out of the Library a longer time than is herein prescribed shal pay into the treasury... for a folio three pence... for a quarto two pence... for an octavo one penny...

Lost Books
If any book belonging to said Library be lost thro the carelessness or neglect of the Proprietor who took the same out thereof, he shall pay for the same into the Treasury so much as said Committe shall judge equitable.

Waiting List for Popular Books
When different Proprietors desire the same book out of the Library at the same time, the Library Keeper shall deliver it to the Proprietor who bids highest for the use of it....

Disorderly Conduct
The said Company shall have power to purge themselves of any disorderly unwholesome member that in a continued course counteracts ye rules & orders herein agreed upon and plainly subverts and hinders the good design of promoting usefull knowledge and Piety...

The Associate Library remained in operation until 1820. The manuscript of its charter now resides in the Connecticut Historical Society and a note on its cover indicates it was presented to the institution by Rev. Erastus Scranton. Scranton was a Yale graduate and in 1805 became the first pastor of the North Milford (later Orange) Ecclesiastical Society. How he acquired the manuscript is unknown but he appears to have been the last member to join the Associate Library, as his signature is the last one found on the list of members. Fortunately, Scranton had the foresight to preserve this historical gem by gifting it to an institution that to this day continues to care for it.

Detail of First Signature Page of the Associate Library Charter
The Connecticut Historical Society, Hartford, Connecticut

Signatories of the Associate Library in Milford

Job Prudden
Noah Baldwin
Joseph Platt
Jonathan Fowller
Edmund Treat
Jonathan Treat
Ephraim Strong
James Norton
Job Clarke
Elihu Sanford
Comfort Hubbell
Peleg Couch (?) Irvin
John Peck
John Treat
Benjamin Prichard
Joseph Treat
Nehemiah Smith
Isaac Clark
Josiah Camp
Enoch Prudden
Andrew Durand
Aaron Fenn
Benjamin Hine
John Prudden
Barnabas Woodcock
Jonathan Prudden
John Down
John Fenn
Jesse Lambert, Jr.
Thomas Welsh
Jeremiah Baldwin
John Durand
Fitch Welch
Solomon Baldwin
John Clark
Joseph Platt
Samuel Prudden
William Powell
Nathan Clark
Sam'el Treat
Ebenezer Batchford
Joseph Whitmore
Edward Allen
Benj. Fenn, Jr.
Nathan Clark
Nathan Brisco
Ephraim Northrup
Thomas Canfield
Joseph Treat
Ebenezer Smith, Jr.
John Plum
John Woodruff
Abigail Ashton
Joseph Sanford
Nathaniel Camp, Jr.
Freelove Weelers
Elias Carrington
Nathaniel Buckingham
Samuel Ford
Nehemiah Woodcock
Lucy Webber
Benjamin Clark
Abel Summers
William Battle

MILFORD *Lost & Found*

Benj. Fenn, Jr.	Richard Platt
Fitch Welch	Elias Carrington, Jr.
Hannah Clark	David Bristol
Enoch Clark	Newton Prudden
Samuel Prudden	Nathan Bristoll
Ann Clark	Jesse P. Lambert
Joseph Robinson	Sam. Higby
Susanna Gunne	Lois Summers
Mary Fenn	Jeremiah Smith
Josiah Sherman	Ebenezer Smith
Sarah Fenn	Benjamin Fenn
William Attwater	Richard Treat, Jr.
Stephen Treat	Sarah Green
Nathan Brisco	Daniel Baldwin
John Ford	David Lombard
Joseph Clark	Richard Fenn
Thankful Baldwin	Caleb Austin
Ephraim Buckingham	Eli Green
Fletcher Prudden	Aaron Fenn
David Fullar	Charles Pruitt
William Fowler	Sarah Treat
Isaac Buckingham	John Ford
Isaac Clarke	Joseph Rogers
Frances Treat	Thomas Ford
Martha Welch	Anne Platt
Susanna Northup	Esther Treat
Wm. Andrews	John Welch
Sam^{el} Humphrevile	Thaddeus Ford
David Treat	Hannah Smith
Jeremiah Bull	John Plumb, Jr.
John Down, Jr.	(Rev.) Erastus Scranton

Connecticut's Sleepy Hollow

"From the listless repose of the place, and the peculiar character of its inhabitants...this sequestered glen has long been known by the name of SLEEPY HOLLOW...A drowsy, dreamy influence seems to hang over the land, and to pervade the very atmosphere... the place still continues under the sway of some witching power, that holds a spell over the minds of the good people, causing them to walk in a continual reverie."

Washington Irving, *The Legend of Sleepy Hollow*, 1819

Sometime after 1819, when Washington Irving first penned his story about Ichabod Crane and the terror that beset him, Milford earned a nickname that seems to have been long forgotten - Sleepy Hollow. Exactly when or why this name became associated with Milford is unclear. In 1838 Edward R. Lambert, a resident of Milford, wrote in his historical work on New Haven colony that "The inhabitants of Milford are mostly farmers, and retain in an eminent degree the manners of the primitive settlers. It being difficult to change long established habits, they are not celebrated for keeping pace with the improvements of the age."[1]

By 1840 the sleepy reputation had become entrenched and was proudly displayed on a banner at a political rally. On February 26, 1840 a meeting of the Whig Young Men of Connecticut was held in Hartford.[2] Five thousand young men descended on the capital city in carriages, by steamboat or rail, on foot or riding on horseback. One thousand men arrived on a train from New Haven. As they marched from the railroad station accompanied by a marching band, one group from Milford sported banners in support of the new presidential nominee and included:

> OLD MILFORD
>
> THEY CALL HER "SLEEPY HOLLOW,"
>
> *She's wide awake for*
>
> HARRISON AND REFORM

That Milford banner wasn't the only one that referred to Washington Irving's home territory. William Henry Harrison's opponent was incumbent President Martin Van Buren of Kinderhook, New York. Irving had actually penned *The Legend of Sleepy Hollow* while staying as a guest at *Lindenwald*, Van Buren's estate in Kinderhook. The banner from North Haven read, "Know, Man of Kinderhook, the People will meet you at the Polls."[3]

Harrison and his vice-presidential running mate John Tyler won the election that year. It was the first national victory for the Whig party, thanks in part to the people of Milford who woke up and supported "Tippecanoe and Tyler Too!" Little did they know they were voting for two presidents in that election. One month after Harrison took the oath of office, he died of pneumonia and John Tyler inherited the reins of government.

Milford's reputation as a sleepy community extended beyond the borders of Connecticut as was evidenced in an article in a Vermont newspaper[4] from 1849 regarding one of Milford's residents:

> Mrs. Anna Northrop, upwards of 80 years of age, a few days since walked from her residence in Milford to the house of a friend in Humphreysville,[5] and returned again the same day having walked a distance of 26 miles, besides knitting, during her visit to the "Ville," two or three inches in length of a stocking! This is a feat, though perhaps common to our revolutionary dames, which would be found difficult to perform by most ladies of the present day. If old Milford has many such smart women as Mrs. N. we protest against the term "Sleepy Hollow" being longer applied to her.

The endearing image of a "Sleepy Hollow" was reinforced when an article on Milford appeared in *New England Magazine* in 1889. The author described Milford, "I suppose a drowsier, lazier town of its size does not exist in all the land of steady habits.[6] The leisurely Spanish custom of taking *siestas* in the middle of the day is followed by the people to an extent which is exceptional, and which would shock the overworked citizens of the great American cities, who do not find the days long enough to do their business in...The reader must not understand *siesta* to be synonymous with nap, however; it is not so understood anywhere. The Milford *siesta*, like that of Andalusia,[7] is simply a time set apart systematically for rest and seclusion during the heat of the day."[8]

Perhaps not so coincidentally, there is actually a strong link between Milford's sleepy reputation and Washington Irving's "Sleepy Hollow" of legend. The well-known tale relates the story of Ichabod Crane, a schoolmaster living in a sleepy community along the Hudson River, and his encounter with the Headless Horseman of Sleepy Hollow. In his story, Washington Irving wrote that Ichabod had moved to Sleepy Hollow from Connecticut:

> In this by-place of nature, there abode, in a remote period of American history, that is to say, some thirty years since, a worthy wight[9] of the name of Ichabod Crane; who sojourned, or, as he expressed it, "tarried," in Sleepy Hollow, for the purpose of instructing the children of the vicinity. He was a native of Connecticut; a State which supplies the Union with pioneers for the mind as well as for the forest, and sends forth yearly its legions of frontier woodsmen and country schoolmasters.[10]

It has long been forgotten that Washington Irving patterned the hapless Ichabod Crane after his friend, Jesse Merwin, who lived in the town of Kinderhook, New York and who was a local schoolmaster. Merwin traced his roots back to Miles Merwin, one of Milford's after-planters, and he himself was born in Milford in 1784. The exact date he moved to Kinderhook is uncertain but in 1808 he is found there, married to Jane Van Dyck with whom he eventually had ten children.

Jesse Merwin
A History of Old Kinderhook

There are two examples of correspondence documenting the Irving - Merwin relationship. One letter from Washington Irving to Jesse Merwin was reprinted in a Boston newspaper in 1851 and is a folksy reminiscence about their lives in Kinderhook. The letter, in part, reads: [11]

...You must excuse me, my good friend Merwin, for suffering your letter to remain so long unanswered...Your letter was indeed most welcome-calling up as it did the recollections of pleasant days passed together in times long since at Judge Van Ness's in Kinderhook...

Do you remember our fishing expedition in company with Congressman Van Allen to the little lake a few miles from Kinderhook; and John Moore, the vagabond admiral of the lake, who sat crouched in a heap in the middle of his canoe in the center of the lake, with fishing rods stretched out in every direction, like the long legs of a spider? And do you remember our piratical prank, when we made up for our bad luck in fishing by plundering his canoe of its fish when we found it adrift? And do you remember how John Moore came splashing along the marsh, roaring at us and how we finished our frolic by driving off and leaving the congressman to John Moore's mercy; tickling ourselves with the idea of his being scalped at least?...

...You told me the old school-house is torn down and a new one built in its place. I am sorry for it. I should have liked to see the old school-house once more, where after my morning's literary task was over, I used to come and wait for you occasionally, until school was dismissed, and you used to promise to keep back the punishment of some little, tough, broad-buttoned Dutch boy until I should come, for my amusement – but never kept your promise. I don't think I should look with a friendly eye on the new school-house, however nice it might be...

MILFORD *Lost & Found*

Jesse Merwin's Cottage in Kinderhook
A History of Old Kinderhook

Whereas the first letter documents the long, strong friendship of Washington Irving and Jesse Merwin, the second letter makes it perfectly clear that Merwin was the inspiration for the hapless Ichabod Crane. Former President Martin Van Buren wrote a letter of introduction[12] for Merwin when he went to New York City to collect money for the Methodist Church in Kinderhook. Van Buren wrote in 1846:

> *This is to certify that I have known J. Merwin, Esq.*
> *of Kinderhook for about 3^d of a century, & believe*
> *him to be a man of honour & integrity; and that he is the*
> *same person celebrated in the writings of the Hon.*
> *Washington Irving under the character of Ichabod Crane in*
> *his famous 'Legend of Sleepy Holow.'*
>
> *M. Van Buren*

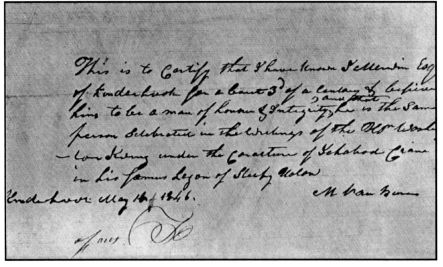

Letter from Martin van Buren
A History of Old Kinderhook

Whether Milford's old moniker "Sleepy Hollow" can be directly related to the Jesse Merwin/Washingon Irving friendship or was simply a nickname bestowed on a quiet, rural community may never be known. It is likely the Milford Merwins kept track of their relative in Kinderhook and his friendship with Washington Irving. Whether the Merwin family bestowed the name Sleepy Hollow on Milford because the "real" Ichabod Crane was actually born and raised there is uncertain. What is known for certain is that the lazy, sleepy reputation of a town unwilling to change has been lost, for many good reasons, with the passage of time.

The Headless Horseman Pursuing Ichabod Crane
Painting by John Quidor, 1858
Courtesy of the Smithsonian American Art Museum
(Museum purchase made possible in part by the Catherine Walden Myer Endowment, the Julia D. Strong Endowment, and the Director's Discretionary Fund.)

MILFORD *Lost & Found*

Past Tents on Welch's Point

The Civil War had begun a few months earlier. In the third week of July 1861, the Union Army was defeated at the Battle of Bull Run. While the Confederacy basked in the glory of its first victory the Union became spurred to win the conflict. Around the country, groups of men and barely men volunteered to join the ranks of the Union. They came from every bend and corner of the North to join the cause.

Washington to Milford Route
J. H. Colton's *Map of Connecticut*, 1854

One morning in August of that same year a group of young men and women in Connecticut, led by able and dedicated leaders, prepared for their own march to the sea. They loaded wagons with provisions to last two weeks – tents and clothing, straw-filled mattresses and blankets, foodstuff and casks of water, and fishing poles to help catch more food if needed. Their leader packed a bugle for reveille and carefully stowed a small cannon into one of the wagons.

The group of some sixty inspired individuals departed the small town of Washington, Connecticut located a few miles southwest of Litchfield. Their exact route is uncertain but they likely followed the nearby Shepaug River south to the Housatonic River and continued toward its mouth in Long Island Sound. For two days, they wended their way through the hills, valleys and towns along the route. Not a regimented group, they could be heard laughing, shouting and singing as they marched along. Eventually their trek became easier as they approached the lowlands nearer the coast. They maneuvered toward the harbor at Milford and beyond, following the shoreline until they reached their destination on Welch's Point. From there, they held a commanding view of ships sailing and steaming through Long Island Sound and of the shoreline to the west. Charles Island, which acted as a natural sentry guarding the approach to the heart of Milford, was clearly within their sights.

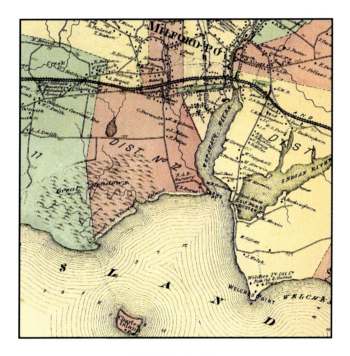

Welch's Point
F. W. Beers' *Atlas of New Haven County*, 1868

But this group of sixty hearty souls was not part of any military campaign. They had not come here to stand sentinel for Connecticut's coastline, nor to join a larger group of Connecticut volunteers in the burgeoning civil war. Rather, they were about to make history in their own right. They had spent weeks of preparation and two days hiking to Milford in order to go camping.

Frederick W. Gunn
Courtesy of
The Gunnery Archives

The leader of this group, Frederick W. Gunn, was a direct descendant of one of Milford's earliest settlers. Jasper Gunn was one of the original 44 freeplanters in Milford in 1639 and held several positions in the new settlement, perhaps best known as being Milford's first physician. He was later appointed sealer of weights and measures, a position of considerable trust as he was responsible for ensuring that traders and merchants were kept honest in representing the weight and volume of their goods. Gunn was also the community's first teacher and he schooled local children at his home near the head of Milford harbor as far back as 1642.

Following in the footsteps of his Milford ancestor, Frederick Gunn and his wife Abigail Brinsmade Gunn founded a private school in Washington, Connecticut in 1850. Gunn had taught for several years in Washington, New Preston and in Towanda, Pennsylvania. After his marriage to Abigail in 1848, they returned to Washington and decided to open a coeducational school, which they named The Gunnery. The school was designed to prepare students for college and that first year twelve students were under its roof.

The Gunnery was founded on four principles – intellectual strength, moral courage, physical rigor and character. As such, the classroom extended beyond the four walls of the school. "As he created his own kind of school, he creatively structured, and very skillfully wove together, sports, nature and camping into his school's curriculum."[13] Gunn's view of developing the whole person was perhaps revolutionary in his day but it likely led to the long term success of the school. Before long, The Gunnery attracted students from around the United States and from foreign nations.

In 1861, as part of the curriculum to develop physical rigor and to commune with nature, Gunn decided to evacuate the school and take the entire student body and faculty on a camping trip to Milford. There may have been another motive for Mr. Gunn. He was an ardent abolitionist and viewed the civil war as an opportunity for his students to join the moral cause. As such, he started to emphasize military-type training for the young men. He was once quoted as saying, "...if I cannot go to the war, I will do my best to make warriors."[14] During the war years and for some time after, the school took on some aspects of a military school and some of this influence was carried over to the camping trips.

Tent Erected on The Gunnery Campus
Courtesy of The Gunnery Archives

The students referred to their camping excursions as "gypsying," not a new word but an aptly descriptive one to describe their outdoor adventure. Weeks of preparation and practice preceded their excursion to Milford.

When the long anticipated day of departure finally arrived the entire school emptied and started the long forty mile trek. One student recalled:

> It was an eventful and joyous day when the loaded wagons, the donkeys, and the long troop of boys and girls dressed in all the hues of the rainbow, began their seaward march down the river road making the old woods echo with laughter and song. For thirty miles the journey took us through the bold valleys of the Shepaug and Housatonic, along a shaded road cut from the hills and giving at every turn some new scene of beauty through the long river vistas. At night we camped in two or three big tents, and the close of the second day found us settled down at the Point, with the salt waves breaking on the bluff a few rods away. It was a jocund ten days that followed, with its sport in the surf, its evening songs, its dances on the turf by night, its ball games, and its touches of more tender sentiment in the moonlight…[15]

Welch's Point Camp in 1863
Mr. Gunn in the center holding his hat
Courtesy of The Gunnery Archives

Camping at Welch's Point, 1861
Note the boys dressed in military-type uniforms
Courtesy of The Gunnery Archives

Emphasizing their military orientation, another student wrote, "...we were voted for our excellent drilling. Who of us that belonged to that company can never forget, when we marched through the towns and villages on our way to camp at Milford beach, how the natives applauded us; our marching was the best ever; the seventh New York was not in it by comparison."[16] Frederick Gunn would wake his campers to reveille on his bugle and then address his captive company about camping in the outdoors and living in the wilderness. "There at our ease, in all positions imaginable, we would sit and listen to the words of advice and caution from Mr. Gunn."[17] He knew the value of training his students to be leaders and organized the camp with a committee of boys who would organize the rest of the group in terms of carrying out camp chores. Gunn's system of providing leadership responsibilities for the older campers was the forerunner to the role of camp counselors today.

Relatively few details exist about the excursions to Milford, other than a few writings by Gunnery students. Mid-19th century newspapers wouldn't have covered an event that didn't seem particularly historic at the time. But, one near tragic incident during one of Gunn's outings in Milford did make it into newsprint. During the camping trip of 1865 there was an accident that was nearly catastrophic:

> While the boys belonging to the school of Mr. F.W. Gunn, of Washington, Ct., which is now encamped at Welch's Point, Milford, were firing a salute on Saturday, the cannon burst, throwing the fragments through the crowd standing around and causing a general stampede. One ragged chunk of iron weighing several pounds was thrown over one tent and through another, making a large rent, and striking in startling proximity to the head of a sleeping boy. Very fortunately nobody was hurt.[18]

This near disastrous event appears to have been memorialized in the name of the school newspaper in 1884 when the *Stray Shot* was introduced on the Gunnery campus. When describing the intent and scope of the new publication, the editor wrote:

> We may seem bold in contributing Stray Shot to the volley of printed matter which the great guns of journalism continually pour forth. If so, the only excuse we can offer for audaciously entering a field already so crowded with heavier artillery, is that certain targets, unheeded by abler marksmen and *temptingly within range of even defective and rude Gunnery weapons* challenge us to fire an occasional bullet-in of news concerning Gunnery affairs...[19]

Today, the name lives on as the title of the school's annual literary journal. Another tradition started in 1959 when the editor of the *Stray Shot* donated a 200 pound cannon ball to the student body for a game of hide-and-seek of sorts. Every year, Gunnery seniors hide the cannonball somewhere on campus and leave clues for junior class members to find it. Once they recover it, they carve their initials into the cannonball, hide it and create clues for the next group of upcoming seniors. Since the start of this tradition, the cannonball has been referred to as The Stray Shot.

After 1865 the venue for gypsying moved to Point Beautiful at Lake Waramaug, seven miles from the school. The overnight camping excursions continued until 1874. Today, The Gunnery pays tribute to its founder's love of the outdoors. Each autumn the students, faculty, and staff go on a hike to Steep Rock Reservation, a few miles from the campus.

Frederick Gunn is the recognized founder of organized camping. After his expeditions to Welch's Point in Milford and later to Lake Waramaug, the first YWCA camp was founded in 1874 in Asbury Park, New Jersey. Two years later, the first private camp was founded and in 1885 the first YMCA camp in New York State opened in Newburgh. These camps, and organized camps ever since, maintain many of the same traditions that began when Frederick and Abigail Gunn brought their students to Milford.

In 1986, the American Camp Association organized a celebration of Gunn's accomplishment. On July 7th a group of 85 campers reenacted the Gunnery students' trek from Washington to Milford and were allowed to camp on Gulf Beach. They were joined by an estimated 1,200 campers from around the United States, who set up camps at various points around Milford. In the evening they all joined activities on Gulf Beach including a campfire fueled by 43 different types of wood brought by campers from points around the United States, games, skits, story-telling, and camp songs led by Paul Stookey of the singing group Peter Paul and Mary.

According to the local newspaper, the event was to be commemorated with a buried time capsule left for a future generation of campers to uncover. The *Milford Citizen* reported, "At 8 p.m. a granite monument with a plaque will be erected and a time capsule containing memorabilia from the city of Milford and the American Camping Association will be buried in honor of the anniversary of Gunn's trip."[20] The next day's paper[21] gave a slightly different account for the time capsule's burial:

> Later in the week a monument will be erected and a time capsule buried on the beach to commemorate Gunn's contribution to camping. In the time capsule, which is scheduled to be opened in 75 years, will be a videocassette of last night's activities, a letter from Mayor Alberta Jagoe to her successor 75 years from now, a few other letters from leaders of the American Camping Association, and a Milford calendar for 1986.

Efforts to locate the granite marker have come up with nothing...no one can recall its location and some speculate it may have been stolen. More troublesome, there is no indication where the time capsule was buried...if it was buried...a good example of how quickly history can be lost. Perhaps some historian will take up this challenge and unearth the time capsule in the distant future.

Girls' Tent on Welch's Point
Courtesy of The Gunnery Archives

Milford 31, Bulldogs 0

It was a cold November day in 1906 and the Yale Bulldogs opposed the Harvard Crimson in what was traditionally called "The Game." An estimated 22,000 of the 32,000 rooters arrived in New Haven by trains. In addition to the regular Pullman service, nine coach trains and six parlor car trains arrived from New York City with a total of 154 additional cars. Five special trains were sent from Boston via the shoreline route; other coaches carrying Crimson fans steamed south from Springfield. Hartford alone sent forty-four trains to New Haven that day.

Most of the other attendees walked, hopped a trolley, traveled by horse-drawn carriage or rode in automobiles. Travel by auto was still a spectacle and attracted the attention of everyone. So many automobiles rolled into New Haven that the streets became clogged and made crossing them difficult. The frenzied scene and early tailgate parties were described by one reporter, "The auto parties began to arrive…and from the big Panhard which bore a party of New York brokers who had given up the session on the exchange to be present at the kickoff to the little 5-horsepower machine which carried three people one and all breezed up Chapel Street on their way to the field where they took their positions in the parking spaces and unstrapped their lunch which they ate leisurely, finishing in plenty of time for the game. There were never so many autos here and it was all one's life was worth to cross the street."[22]

The two teams lined up shortly after 2:00 that afternoon. The local newspaper reported, "The fate of Yale-Harvard football hung in the balance while the old rivals surged over the chalk-lines with 32,000 spectators cheering the ebb and flow of the battle in a feverish excitement unequalled in any game in New Haven history."[23] This was a pivotal year for football. The American Football Rules Committee headed up by the sire of American football, Walter Camp, instituted many changes to reduce the brutality of the game. Prior to these new rules, brute force was more important than skill on the gridiron. The changes included the "ten-yard rule" that required a team to make ten yards in three downs. Formerly, players were required to make only five yards in three downs. For the first time in college football history the forward pass was legalized during this season, as was the on-side kick. Also, the line of scrimmage was defined as two separate lines – both parallel with the goal line – passing through both ends of the football. This created a narrow no-man's land for the two teams.

This was the first time Yale and Harvard would clash under the new rules of engagement established a few months earlier. The newspaper article continued, "That the new rules were to receive their supreme test was almost an incidental feature to the supreme intensity of the maddening desire to win by both the elevens."[24] New rules or not, the two teams faced off in "The Game" as they had every year since 1875. Both teams attempted the forward pass with varying degrees of success and one of the passes resulted in a touchdown for Yale. The Bulldogs proved to be the victors that day beating the Crimson with a score of 6 to 0.

New rules were not only being enforced in football. Speeding autoists had begun to become a statewide problem. As the speed of automobiles increased and the quality of roads improved, drivers often pushed their cars to the limit. It had only been the previous year that the state legislature revamped the laws relating to automobiles. New laws related to the registration of vehicles, displaying license plates, sharing the road, use of lights on vehicles, etc. One law required autos to come to a complete stop if a horse on the road became scared. The speed limit laws were also modified. The legal maximum speed was increased to 12 mph in the cities and 20 mph in the country. The penalties for violating the speed laws were stiff. For a first offense the driver could be fined $25 to $200 or spend up to 30 days in jail. A second offense could double the fine or jail time.

In October of 1906 the Milford town fathers voted, "that it is the sense of this meeting that the selectmen and prosecuting officers of the town take such steps, as are necessary, to have the statute laws concerning the Registration, Numbering, Use and Speed of motor vehicles strictly be enforced within the town limits."[25] It was obvious some action was needed to show the public that the town was serious about enforcing the motor vehicle laws. The local constable was given the responsibility to put teeth into the new directive. He wasted no time and on October 8th he charged ten drivers with speeding violations. With his confidence high and his technique for catching speeders refined, he continued to enforce the speed laws.

Automobilists heading to The Game in New Haven from the west traveled the Boston Post Road and many of them hurried in anticipation of the contest and the hoopla associated with it. Unknown to them, a surprise awaited along the road in Milford. Constable James M. Maher, Officer Mortimer B. Fowler and Deputy Sheriff Mallory were hiding behind a small barn along the roadway, armed with stopwatches. They had measured the distance between two points along the road and calculated how long it should take an automobile to travel the distance at the proper speed. One-by-one the cars drove the route and one-by-one those found to be speeding were stopped. Constable Maher simply stepped out from his hiding place behind the barn and flagged them down. That day, thirty-one drivers were netted in violation of the new speeding law.

Boston Post Road at Naugatuck Ave., Milford (c. 1908)
Courtesy of DeForest W. Smith

Maher and his assistants collected a cash bond of $25 from each violator and obtained their promise to appear in court the following Monday, or the bond would be forfeited. Most of those pulled over claimed they were innocent and vowed to fight the charge. Caught in the act were several well-known personages including lawyer and State Senator Allan W. Paige of Bridgeport. When the constable learned his identity he offered to let him go. Incensed that he should be granted a special privilege not offered to the others, Paige insisted he pay the bond and planned to appear in court "to make it warm for the officers."[26]

Mrs. Eugenia Herreshoff, wife of the famous, blind yacht-builder John Brown Herreshoff of Bristol, Rhode Island was also caught that morning. She was driving in a "large canopy-top machine"[27] with two other ladies from New York and claimed she was driving at a very slow pace. She explained she was of a "nervous temperament...and could not stand running the auto at more than half the speed the law allows."[28] Despite her pleas of innocence, she was promptly arrested and ordered to appear in court.

Mrs. Herreshoff told a markedly different story to a Newport newspaper than was reported locally. Apparently embarrassed by the incident she related an account intended to gain sympathy from the readers. The newspaper reported that a robber jumped in front of her car in Milford and stopped her. He identified himself as James Maher, told her he was a constable, informed her she had been speeding and that she was being fined $25. She denied the charge and after Maher threatened her with arrest she paid the fine. Herreshoff claimed she reported the incident to Newport police and learned that "she was the victim of the newest game in highway robbery to which automobilists are subjected." The news article continued, "Up to a late hour last evening "Maher" had not been arrested. He is not known to the police in Milford or New Haven."[29]

The violators were angry and accused the town of sponging off those who drove through. Yet, twenty-six of them forfeited their bonds without further argument, quickly netting $650 for the town. The speed trap was not the only one conducted that day. North of New Haven police netted many other Yale-Harvard autoists. These enforcement activities caught the attention of many newspapers and the *New Haven Evening Register* wrote an editorial[30] about the speed traps:

THE AUTOMOBILE ARRESTS

It is difficult to understand the wholesale arrests which were made by town officials to the north and south of New Haven last Saturday of automobilists, who were on their way to and from the Yale-Harvard football game. Doubtless there were many, who in their eagerness to reach the city, exceeded the speed limit law, but the reports in the newspapers do not in all instances by any means make it clear that the autoists were abusing the highways and endangering life.

The conflict appears to be between over zealous town officials, on the one hand and over zealous autoists on the other hand. The determination upon the part of the former to give all their time to the detection of autoing sinners may have led them to take a greater interest in making arrests and imposing punishments than the facts called for…

… Something should be said, however, of the autoist who cares nothing for the laws of the state and who holds in contempt the well known rules of the road. He is fortunately not in the majority…As a rule the drivers who use the road do so with a full regard for the rights of the highway and for the rights of the people…This of itself should stimulate town officials to act in a conservative spirit and not in a radical spirit as many of them acted last Saturday.

Nine years later, the very well-known Constable James Maher, who so carefully noted the times on his stopwatch that November morning, became Milford's first Chief of Police. Officer Mortimer Fowler, who hid behind the barn with Maher, became Milford's second police chief in 1931.

James Maher
Milford's First Police Chief

Courtesy of Robert L. Berchem
and
Milford Police Department

Charles Hobby Pond's Island View
Courtesy of Academy of Our Lady of Mercy, Lauralton Hall

For the Love of Laura

There is a little island within the city limits of Milford that is home to one of Milford's treasures. This peaceful, landlocked oasis is almost hidden away from the rest of the town. Every day thousands of people drive by its gated grounds and barely pay any attention to it. Located on High Street, a short distance from the Milford Green, it is home to a Catholic girls' school formally known as the Academy of Our Lady of Mercy.

Its history dates back to 1864 when Charles Hobby Pond (b. October 11, 1833) and his wife Mary built the home where they would raise their family. The Pond family was well-known around Milford. Charles Pond's great uncle, also Charles Hobby Pond, was Lieutenant Governor of Connecticut under Governor Thomas Hart Seymour. When Seymour was appointed Minister to Russia by President Pierce he resigned his position in Hartford. The elder Pond became governor of Connecticut for a few months in 1853 – 1854.

The younger Charles H. Pond and his bride built a twenty-room, granite, Victorian-Gothic mansion. It needed to be large for their six children – Mary, Matilda, Bessie, Winthrop, Florence and Charles – and their domestic staff. From the mansion's single, square tower the family enjoyed a view of Charles Island and Pond named his new home Island View.

Charles Pond ran into financial troubles, lost much of his fortune, and died in 1881 at the young age of 47 years. His wife Mary continued to reside in the mansion with her children until 1884 when she leased it to Henry Augustus Taylor. In 1889, he purchased the property outright as a summer residence. His primary residence was in New York City at 11 West Forty-sixth Street. Taylor was a New York banker and had made considerable wealth constructing and investing in railroads in Iowa, Minnesota, New York, Ohio, and Wisconsin. He married Mary Anna Meyer in 1865 and they had seven children, of whom three died at birth or an early age. Mary Taylor died in 1878, probably related to complications from the birth of their son Lawrence, who died about the same time.

Henry A. Taylor then married Elizabeth Prudence Conrey in 1880. Together they had an additional six children, two of whom died at an early age. When Taylor purchased Island View from Mary Pond in 1889 he decided to re-christen the estate with the name Lauralton Hall. Exactly who Taylor had in mind as the namesake is a matter of some debate. His mother was named Laura (Thomas) Taylor; his sister was Laura (Taylor) Sandford; and his daughter, Laura Peters Taylor was born in 1883 and died in 1888 – the year before Taylor named his estate. Although he may well have honored three generations of Laura Taylors, the recent loss of his daughter and a remembrance Taylor incorporated into a local church a few years later provide evidence that he named the estate Lauralton Hall after his recently deceased daughter.

Taylor made several architectural changes to the main house. The most prominent feature was the addition of a round tower with leaded glass windows providing expansive views. He re-designed and greatly enlarged the colonnaded veranda and added a porte cochere, allowing a protective cover for people alighting from their coaches. On the interior he constructed an elaborate, mahogany, three-story, circular staircase topped by a stained-glass skylight. The craftsmen who built the staircase used no nails in its construction; it was assembled using only wooden pegs.

Two significant buildings in Milford carry the Taylor name and were generous gifts to the community from the family. The Methodist church, located on River Street since 1842, was in search of property on which to build a new house of worship. Henry A. Taylor got wind of their efforts and on April 15, 1891 invited the pastor, Rev. James A. Macmillan, to meet with him at Lauralton Hall. Taylor made him an offer that would have been difficult to refuse. He offered the pastor property along the town green for a new church that would be named for his late wife and that would be donated by their children. In honor of their mother, Mary (Meyer) Taylor, her four surviving children – John Howard, Margharita, Mary Elizabeth, and Henry Augustus - donated the new church on Broad Street.

Henry Taylor's Lauralton Hall
Courtesy of Academy of Our Lady of Mercy, Lauralton Hall

Dedicated on June 25, 1893 the Mary Taylor Memorial Methodist Episcopal Church (now the Mary Taylor Memorial United Methodist Church) also honored one of Henry's children from his second marriage. A stained glass window displaying a lovely image of an angel was placed in the church in memory of Laura Peters Taylor (see frontispiece). A second window can be found directly opposite Laura's angel. It is considerably simpler in design with Alpha and Omega symbols as its dominant design features. In the lower portion of the stained glass is the name Henry Johns Taylor. Popular belief is that the name refers to either Laura's brother or to one of the deceased children from Henry Taylor's first marriage. Laura's brothers were named Washington and Bayard. The deceased brothers of the four Taylor children who donated the church were named Christopher, Lawrence and John Henry. It is probable the window was dedicated to Henry Augustus Taylor's father – Henry Johns Taylor (1815-1889) who had been mayor of Jersey City and was later a member of the New Jersey state legislature. The church is really a tribute to three generations of Taylors – Henry A. Taylor's wife Mary, his father Henry, and his daughter Laura.

Two of Henry A. Taylor's Children
Courtesy of Academy of Our Lady of Mercy, Lauralton Hall

In 1893, Henry Augustus Taylor announced that he wanted to donate a new library to the town of Milford. The town acquired a piece of property at the corner of Broad and River Streets and Taylor donated $25,000 to build the beautiful granite and stone structure. Part of the agreement required the town to provide $1,000 per year for the building's maintenance for fifty years. Memorial shelves were built and descendants of many of Milford's earliest families donated books to establish the original collection and to memorialize their ancestors. The Henry A. Taylor Library was dedicated on February 2, 1895.

Henry Augustus Taylor
Courtesy of the City of Milford

Although Taylor was recognized as a successful businessman and generous philanthropist, all was not so successful with his private life. He and his second wife, Elizabeth, separated and in 1890 he obtained a divorce based on what he claimed to be his wife's intemperance. Elizabeth unsuccessfully challenged the divorce claiming it had been fraudulently obtained and was null and void.[31] Their two older daughters – Elinor and Henrietta - continued to reside with Henry but eventually moved to St. Petersburg to live with Henry's daughter Margharita who had married Russian Count Nicolas de Chraporitsky. But the youngest child, Bayard, lived with his maternal grandmother.

After Henry A. Taylor's death in 1899 fighting started over his $20,000,000 estate. Taylor's former mother-in-law, Margaret Conrey of New York, claimed she had been raising Taylor's son Bayard since her daughter's divorce and wanted compensation from the estate.

> "The boy's grandmother…is seeking to get an allowance of $7 a week for his care. Mrs. Conery also has another suit against the administrators of the estate, who are children of the first wife, for $5000 for the care she has taken of the child in the past. Mrs. Conrey is devoted to the boy and fears that he may be taken from her."[32]

The estate administrators weren't against supporting 11-year old Bayard but they felt he should reside with members of the Taylor family and not with his maternal grandmother. Mrs. Conrey contended that Henry Taylor's home had not been a good place for the boy to be raised when Taylor was alive for a variety of reasons. These included her accusation that Henry Taylor maintained a "loose and immoral life." She claimed he had an ongoing affair with his housekeeper, Louise Duvernoy, and they had children as a result. There is evidence this story has validity. According to census records[33] and Louise Duvernoy's obituary[34] Louise gave birth to a son, Colombus Henry Taylor, in New York about 1893. Interestingly, Louise went by the surname Taylor, raising the possibility she either adopted the name of her son's father or was secretly married to Henry Taylor.

Henry Taylor's housekeeper was the fourth person in his will to be mentioned – immediately after two of his sons and his son-in-law. It was only after he took care of his housekeeper that Taylor left portions of his estate to the rest of his children. Taylor bequeathed $20,000 to her, an amount worth over $1,000,000 in today's dollars. His will reads in part:

> "I give and bequeath…to Louise Catherine Duvernoy, who is at present a member of my household acting as my housekeeper, said sum of Twenty thousand dollars to be acknowledged by said Louise Catherine Duvernoy to be in full for all services rendered me and in full for all claims and demands against my estate by her."

MILFORD *Lost & Found*

According to a news account of the court proceedings Henry A. Taylor, Jr. testified that Louise Duvernoy, "had stated in a deposition taken in New York that she was married to his father."[35] This secret marriage may well have been true. Throughout the rest of her life, Louise Duvernoy was known as Louise C. Taylor, moved to California with her son, and died there in 1953.

The wrangling over the custody and child support for Bayard Taylor ended. The Taylor property on High Street in Milford was vacated and the administrators of the estate decided to put Lauralton Hall up for sale. Instead of being sold to another wealthy banker or industrialist, the property eventually attracted the attention of a religious order that was firmly established in Connecticut. The Sisters of Mercy had been founded in Ireland by Catherine McAuley in 1831. A contingent of sisters first came to the United States in 1843 to minister to the sick and the poor, and to build and staff schools.

Entrance Hall at Base of the Circular Staircase
Courtesy of Academy of Our Lady of Mercy, Lauralton Hall

Academy of Our Lady of Mercy with the new St. Joseph Building, c. 1906
Courtesy of Academy of Our Lady of Mercy, Lauralton Hall

Shortly after the start of the twentieth century the sisters at St. Bridget's Convent in Meriden decided to build a school. They envisioned a convent school for young women and started searching for suitable properties. The Mother Superior, Reverend Mother Mary Augustine Claven, was offered a property that suited their needs in Southington on the grounds of St. Thomas Church bordering Bristol and Eden Avenues. Rev. William Doolan, rector of the parish, gave the Sisters of Mercy the deed to a 6-acre parcel of land adjoining church property. The property had a handsome house, meadow, woods, and a pond. One small problem was the old St. Thomas Cemetery was also located there. In April and May of 1903 Father Doolan arranged for the bodies to be disinterred and reburied at the new cemetery on Meriden Avenue, clearing the way for the new school.

The Academy of Our Lady of Mercy was all set to have a home. Then, second thoughts and influences from another part of the state began to have an effect on their decision. Some felt the new school would be too close to Mount St. Joseph's Academy in West Hartford and would draw from the same population. The Sisters of Mercy also maintained schools in Meriden, Middletown, Lakeville and Putnam but had none in southern Connecticut. Another problem was there was no access by train to the Southington site, a problem in a day when automobiles weren't widespread. Rev. Peter H. McLean of St. Mary's Parish in Milford had long wanted to establish a secondary school along the coast and knew the Taylor estate was available. It also happened to reside about a quarter mile from the railroad station.

The Taylor family wanted $37,500 for the property but the Sisters of Mercy had a strict budget of $35,000. Negotiations among Father McLean, Reverend Mother Mary Augustine and members of the Taylor family were finally successful with one proviso; that the name Lauralton Hall be retained. This country estate, including the mansion, stables, icehouses, greenhouses, graperies, six smaller houses, and forty acres was transferred to the new owners on January 18, 1905.

Improvements to the property costing about $25,000 were made in order to prepare it as an elementary and secondary school that would accommodate 200 young women. The school opened on September 11,

1905 with an initial enrollment of twenty-five girls. Lauralton Hall opened as a boarding school and had a large number of day students from the surrounding communities. Today, the Academy of Our Lady of Mercy is a thriving school in Milford. It still maintains the name Lauralton Hall in remembrance of a young girl who forever had a special place in her father's heart.

**The Little Girl in the Foreground
is likely Laura Peters Taylor**
Courtesy of Academy of Our Lady of Mercy, Lauralton Hall

Sahara Sands on Smith's Point

People who know Milford don't often think of it as having a desert but that wasn't always the case. One silent film company decided that part of Milford had just the right characteristics to represent a desert scene. The year was 1915. Movies were coming into their own as an art form but movie companies didn't always have the funds to film on location. Feature Film Corporation and Director Edward Jose decided to bring Rudyard Kipling's *The Light that Failed* to the silver screen. This was the first Kipling story to be made into a film. Kipling had reservations about allowing his writings to be portrayed on the screen; he felt the cinema was "too new and immature."[36] He was asked to write the subtitles for this production and subsequently allowed it to be produced.

Kipling's small novel had been published in 1890 and related the story of Dick Heldar, an artist in the Sudan, who was in love with his foster sister Maisie. His affections were unrequited and he had begun to lose his sight from a sword wound he had obtained in the Sudan. Depressed over the loss of love and light, he struggled feverishly to finish his last painting – *Melancholia* – before his sight failed him altogether. Spurned by his lover, Heldar vowed to die fighting at the war front. Even when Maisie is contacted to come to him and told that he was likely to die, she left him to his fate. Probably feeling that Kipling's ending wasn't dramatic enough, the filmmakers re-wrote the final scene and showed Maisie rushing to the battlefront to be with the man she

Robert Edeson
Studio Photo

loved. During the final battle sequence the two died in each other's arms.

Popular stage actor Robert Edeson had made the transition to the silent screen and was cast as Heldar; he reportedly was paid $2,000 a week for his performance. Jose Collins played Bessie the model, Lillian Tucker was Maisie, and Claude Fleming was cast as Heldar's friend Torpenhow.

Jose Collins
Studio Photo

One thing the director needed was a desert setting. The beach on Smith's Point was selected as best resembling the deserts in Northern Africa. Why, one might rightfully ask, would a film director use Connecticut's shoreline with winter lurking around the corner as representing a desert? It appears that the Barnum & Bailey Circus was wintering in Bridgeport, and besides sand, the filmmaker was also in need of camels and Arabian horses.[37] The good folks at Barnum & Bailey willingly supplied them.

During the weeks that preceded filming, advertisements were placed in area newspapers searching for extras to be in the movie. They were compensated $2.50 per day. It was mistakenly reported in some out-of-area newspapers that the filming took place at Fayerweather Island off Bridgeport. Though the film company may have considered that location, the newspapers in Bridgeport and Hartford both described the action as taking place on the beaches of Milford.

On December 13, 1915 a caravan of actors, extras, circus animals and filmmakers invaded Milford and descended on Smith's Point. After the tide had gone out, and with about 100 Milford residents watching, filming began. The beach was turned into a battleground with some 250 actors. To preserve the realistic look of the desert, the cameras were positioned so the water of Long Island Sound was always out of view. One news account[38] described the action:

> The camera operators trained their machines on the stretch of sand at Smith's Point and were careful of course that their focus did not take in any part of Long Island sound for water wouldn't be a good thing to show in the middle of a desert. There were three companies of militia, about 100 men dressed as Arabs, or something of that sort, and about fifteen camels taking part in the scene. Anyway the two parties met on the sand and they had an awful fight with all sorts of heavy gunwork. Bob Edeson was blind, for the purposes of the picture, and was being led around by a little dog...when the shouting was all over the soldiers and the Arabs lay around on the sand about three deep and it appears that everybody had been killed except Edeson. Even the little dog he had relied upon as his guide had been killed...

The filmmakers had forgotten to take into account that weather in Connecticut would be quite cold in December. The actors hadn't. After the big battle scene was finished the director realized that many of the soldiers had worn gloves during the entire time they were on camera. One of the directors was furious and yelled, "Who in h___ ever wore gloves on a broiling desert?"[39] The entire scene with all the actors – soldiers, Arabs, extras, horses, camels and a dog - had to be re-shot; this time with the soldiers barehanded. Director Edward Jose reminded the actors, "Remember men. You are fairly shriveling from intense heat! You are parched, exhausted and dripping perspiration. You must register all that!"[40] Even the director was suffering from the cold and as he spoke his teeth "chattered like castanets."[41]

There was one other problem. During a close-up of Robert Edeson, the director noticed vapor as Edeson breathed. "Heaven! This will never do in a desert scene! Mr. Edeson, you must hold your breath."[42] In addition, all the actors were told to hold their breath when on camera so the desert scene would look realistic. Fortunately, the film crew and actors finished filming in Milford that day, for that night and all the next day the state was hit with a major blizzard, the worst since the big one of 1888.[43]

Two weeks after the problems encountered on the beaches of Milford Robert Edeson was interviewed about the future of motion pictures. "The screen is a strange medium. There is no tomorrow in the movies; each day brings its own problems, and as they are solved the art moves constantly to a higher plane. Interest in pictures is increasing and will continue to increase. The silent house and the lighted screen have a peculiar fascination and vivid effect on one, and you forget time and place."[44]

Unfortunately, the 1916 version of *The Light that Failed* appears to have been placed in the dustbin of history and no copies of it are known to exist.

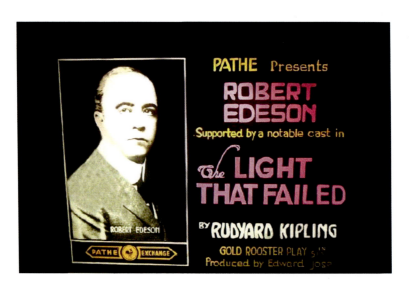

Lantern Slide from *The Light that Failed*
Courtesy of Thomas Hilmer

The Tragic Pajama Parade

The Milford School was a landmark in Milford from its founding in 1916 to its closure in 2002. Located at the corner of Gulf Street and New Haven Avenue, the school was founded by Joseph, Samuel and Harris Rosenbaum. The three brothers were born in Russia, immigrated to New Haven and attended Yale University. While at Yale they started tutoring other students and after graduating they started the Rosenbaum Tutoring School in New Haven in 1908.

The Rosenbaums decided to broaden their educational influence by expanding from a small tutoring facility to a full college preparatory school. They found, "There were more distractions in a college town than was good for the boys. Furthermore, the student body was scattered in New Haven, making it impossible to create any unity or school spirit. Milford was selected as an ideal town for the school, and in September 1916, the school was moved there."[45] They purchased several houses and in 1920, the school acquired the former William S. Pond estate on Gulf Street and named it Milford School. The preparatory academy proved successful and attracted the attention of students nationwide

The students ran into some problems with the local police during one the school's early years in Milford. On the night of September 7, 1920 about fifty students, undoubtedly encouraged by summer faculty members, started what they called a "Pajama Club" and decided to inaugurate the event by participating in a parade through the center of Milford wearing their pajamas. Around 9 o'clock that evening the group assembled on Gulf Street and the festivities began. Singing, ringing bells and blowing horns the young men marched to the town green causing a minor disturbance in the normally quiet community. Marching alongside the students were two members of the faculty – Dr. Royal Nemiah and Dr. Louis Silverman. The Latin and mathematics professors taught at Dartmouth College and were teaching at Milford School for the summer session.

Milford School
The Typhoon, 1922

Some of the town's residents complained to the police that there was a noisy disturbance. Three members of the police force responded to the complaint. What happened next is still somewhat unclear. According to news accounts, as soon as the students saw the police they started running in all directions. The police claimed some students started throwing rocks and one of them reportedly struck Officer Clarence Douglass with a brick (though school officials disputed this). One student ran toward the telephone building on High Street and attempted to climb a fence. Officer Douglass chased the young man and fired his revolver, shooting student Spencer H. Libby, age 20, in the fleshy part of the leg in back of the knee, fortunately missing all his bones.

The crowd quickly dispersed and two students were arrested for breach of peace. One of those arrested was the injured Spencer Libby of Iron River, Michigan and the other was Lee Gimbel, son of the head of Gimbel Brothers Department Stores in New York. The two students were taken to the police headquarters where they were each held on $25 bonds. It was only after he was released from police custody that Libby was treated for his gunshot injury.

Pajama parades had become a custom at several universities and private schools in the 19th and 20th centuries. It was a slightly irreverent activity that was sometimes scorned by school administrators. In 1862 at Union College in Schenectady, the President called a faculty meeting to discuss "a disgraceful exhibition made last evening by 8 or 10 students who showed themselves in front of college about 1 o'clock in their shirts alone. They called themselves the "shirt-tail brigade" and after a series of silly performances and noise retired. So indecent an exhibition, it was thought, should be noticed and if possible stopped."[46]

Sometimes upper classmen forced the freshmen to march in their "jammies" as sort of a hazing ritual. Such was the case at the University of Connecticut[47] where parades were held in which freshmen had to wear only their pajamas, march across the campus singing "How Green We Are," all the while being paddled by sophomores. The pajama parades were stopped in 1925 by the college president because one of the students suffered a spinal injury after being paddled. Pajama parades did sometimes get out-of-hand but most of the time were looked upon as simply good fun.

Dartmouth College, academic home of Professors Nemiah and Silverman, also had its tradition of pajama parades. Dating back to at least 1895, these spectacles were associated with post-game celebratory bonfires and were referred to as "peerades."[48] Usually it was the freshmen who were made to wear pajamas. Sometimes the students marched through the town, other times they did a snake dance around the bonfire clad in their nightwear. In 1925, the freshmen took to burning their pajamas in the bonfire and the campus newspaper wrote, "A flying squadron of sophomores made the rounds of the dormitories…and succeeded in persuading 75 freshmen to secure wood for the fire…the freshmen danced gaily around the blaze until 75 pairs of pajamas were a total loss…"[49] It is likely that Nemiah and Silverman innocently brought Dartmouth's tradition to Milford with them, never anticipating the outcome.

The Milford Pajama Parade was considerably tamer than those held by the older college students at Union College, UConn and Dartmouth yet had met with more tragic results. The day following the Milford shooting the *Bridgeport Post* ran a scathing editorial[50] about the incident:

BAD JUDGMENT

Police officers who use no more judgment than to shoot their revolvers at sky-larking schoolboys, ought certainly not to be entrusted with dangerous weapons. In America, policemen are armed, which is contrary to the custom in many other civilized countries, where the moral force of the officers' uniform – backed by his good right arm where necessary – is usually found sufficient.

But the American policeman has always carried a revolver, perhaps as a heritage of wilder and woollier days. This revolver involves additional discretion on the part of the officer. It is not to be lightly drawn and fired whenever its possessor gets excited. Promiscuous shooting by members of the police force is just as bad as promiscuous shooting by anybody else.

The fact that schoolboys threw stones at the Milford police officers who were pursuing them is no justification for the shooting of one of the boys. If the Milford authorities have any gumption they will see that the officer in question is at once brought up on charges. If he must play with a pistol, give him a cap pistol. The shooting of a schoolboy by a policeman is a disgrace to a civilized community.

After the events of Milford's pajama parade, a police inquiry was held to investigate the events. The head of the school, Dr. Samuel Rosenbaum, threatened the town with a lawsuit, saying the school would "go to the limit."[51] He claimed there was no demonstration on the part of the students that would have caused the reaction from Officer Douglass. He was quoted, "An officer who loses his head as this officer did, and begins to shoot at the slightest provocation is a menace to the town. We have witnesses to prove that this officer who shot one of our students is the same one who drew his revolver on a crowd of little boys eight to ten years of age who were playing craps. Such a man should not be tolerated on the police force."[52]

Rosenbaum's claim of poor judgment was disputed by Milford Police Chief James Maher who claimed that after he asked the group of pajama-clad pupils to return to the school grounds, one of the students threw a rock at him and the students then ran in all directions. It was then that Spencer Libby climbed over a fence to get away and was accidentally shot. "Officer Douglass who has a reputation of being a level headed officer of considerable experience, claims that he had no intention of discharging his pistol; and that, in mounting a fence in the chase, it was accidentally discharged."[53] The *Bridgeport Post* reported, "The entire town of Milford was "aflutter with conversation and rumors and charges and everything."[54]

At the end of the formal inquiry, Officer Douglass was suspended without pay for thirty days. He returned to his Milford Center beat after his suspension period. Breach of peace charges against Libby and Gimbel were nolled, and the threatened lawsuit against the town never transpired. Professors Nemiah and Silverman returned to Dartmouth leaving behind a nearly disastrous attempt at establishing a tradition. What was Milford's first Pajama Parade also seems to have been its last…that is, up until now.

Milford Police Department, c. 1920s
Courtesy of Robert L. Berchem
and
Milford Police Department

Thoroughly Modern Milford

In 1921, Connecticut beachgoers had been testing the rising waters of fashion and exposing a bit more skin than some local people thought proper. Dimpled knees, which had begun to be spotted on Chapel Street in New Haven, were not allowed along the west shore beaches including Milford. Makers of women's bathing garb, which usually included full length stockings in addition to skirts, had even begun (gasp!) to replace the stockings with socks instead. Socks, held up by "pretty be-ribboned elastics"[55] were considerably more revealing and shocked some more modest residents. Other apparel houses had even started selling one-piece bathing suits without skirts or stockings. In Milford, the town wanted to pass an ordinance requiring beachgoers to cover themselves from the shoulders to the knees when going to and from the beach.

The towns along Connecticut's coast weren't the only shoreline communities dealing with this issue. The previous year Coney Island police declared that, "...women entering the Atlantic or lounging on the sand must wear stockings – not socks. One-piece bathing suits are banned and skirts must fall to the knees. And above all, there must be no "shimmying."[56] Atlantic City's Chief of Police had the tough job of going on an inspection trip to the Pacific coast bathing beaches and taking photographs of the various bathing suit styles. He presented his report and photos to Atlantic City's Board of Beach Censors and after carefully scrutinizing the images the board promptly issued an edict that "one-piece bathing suits would

Professional Swimmer
Annette Kellerman
Modeling a Controversial One-Piece Bathing Suit

be permanently barred from the beaches." [57]

Many female bathers were up in arms about Milford's unfair modesty regulation. One woman, who was an accomplished competitive swimmer and diver, stated, "I don't think a woman who goes in swimming wearing a one-piece suit and no stockings attracts any more attention than a woman who goes down the main street wearing a diaphanous frock with a short skirt and transparent stockings. The transparency of her stockings calls more attention to the fact that she has a dimpled knee than her bare limbs would at the shore." [58]

Another woman complained that she "...cannot swim when hampered by a skirt, and feels that it is just as immodest for the men to appear in their bathing costumes as it is for a girl to wear one-piece bathing suits." [59] She continued, "Why are men allowed all the privileges? I can't swim at all with a skirt and what else do I come to the shore for? Last year at Atlantic City they started some of the same sort of nonsense, and now they are starting it here. It's positively dangerous for a woman to be hampered by a skirt and stockings."

Bayview Beauties c. 1920
Courtesy of Joseph Finn

These fashion developments caused quite a stir both at home and in Hartford, where the subject was discussed at the legislative level. The General Assembly granted towns the power to regulate the modesty of attire worn on public streets and beaches and left it up to the individual towns to interpret the meaning of "modest." Although Milford didn't plan to regulate bathing togs on the beach itself the town fathers were concerned that beachgoers walking to and from the beach should be modestly covered. Police Commission President Stanley Clark stated, "…the police do not care what kind of bathing suit adorns the charms of the fair sex as long as the proper outside covering is worn when going to and from the cottages to the water."[60]

Milford's Board of Police Commissioners wanted to pass an ordinance that "no person more than twelve years old shall be on the streets or in public places in a bathing suit unless they wear an outside wrap extending from the shoulders to the knees."[61] The ordinance would apply to "the male sex as well as the fair maids and matrons who frequent Milford beaches."[62] Offenders would be subject to a fine not to exceed fifty dollars.

Picturesque America
Charles Dana Gibson

Several hearings were held on the subject and not one member of the public spoke in favor of the new regulation. One woman from New Haven Avenue in Woodmont thought the ordinance was ridiculous and told the commissioners that "she would be among those arrested for violating the ruling...and came to the shore to enjoy bathing but did not want to be bothered with coats, sweaters or bathrobes while going to and from her cottage."[63] In spite of the opposition the police board passed the regulation in executive session, feeling it was "best for the interest and welfare of the whole public."[64]

Immediately after the police commissioners approved the ordinance, they ordered Milford Chief of Police James Maher to inform his men of the new law and to start enforcing it using their good judgment. One news account concluded, "At any rate there is a law of the state which says that women's bathing apparel must be modest, and town officials may interpret it as they please. Milford having seen fit to cover the bather's knees, there is nothing that can be done about it but pout and cover them. Women at other beaches are hoping no such drastic measures will be taken elsewhere. And so are the men!"[65]

It has not been determined when, or even if, Milford's cover-up ordinance was ever repealed.

"The best material for a bathing costume is flannel, and the most suitable color is gray, and may be trimmed with bright worsted braid. The loose sacque, or the yoke waist, both to be belted in, and falling about midway between the knee and the ankle, is the best form of bathing costume. An oil-skin cap to protect the hair from water, and merino socks to match the dress, complete the costume."

American Etiquette and Rules of Politeness

The Greatest Amusement Sensation

It was approaching eight o'clock on a Friday evening and hundreds of cars filled with occupants streamed up and down Route 1 toward the intersection with Cherry Street. They were all going to see what had been billed as the "Greatest Amusement Sensation in Connecticut."[66] On that 26th night of May 1939, Connecticut's first drive-in movie theater opened to the public in Milford.

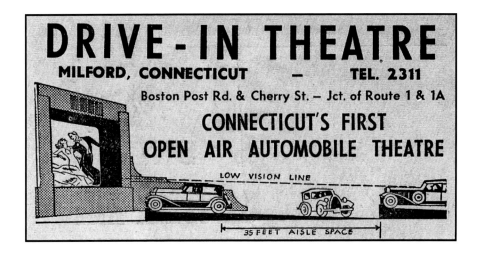

Drive-in theaters were a relatively new phenomenon, the first being opened in Camden, New Jersey during the summer of 1933. The first patent for a drive-in theater[67] was granted to Richard M. Hollingshead, Jr. just a couple of months before the Camden theater opened. Hollingshead's invention incorporated all the elements that would make up drive-in theaters as we know them. In his patent he solved several technical problems. He devised a means for all viewers to see the screen by arranging the parking area in a semi-circular pattern and designing parking ramps that would not obstruct the view of the cars in back.

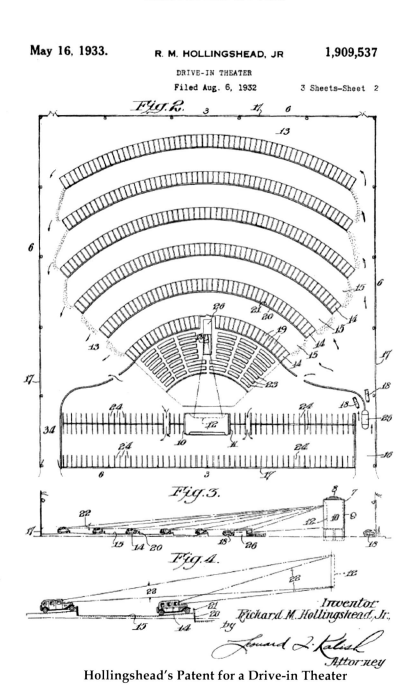

Hollingshead's Patent for a Drive-in Theater

Hollingshead also addressed problems of insects being drawn to the light of the projector and their images being projected onto the screen. He designed a three to six foot funnel to be placed directly in front of the projector lens. Clean air was blown into the end nearest the projector and out the far end. This simple solution successfully prevented insects from approaching the projector's lens.

> **NO PARKING TROUBLES**
> Just drive right in, stay in your car, and enjoy our shows!
> Your car, parked in the theatre, offers all the advantages of a private box. Any type of dress is correct at the Drive-In Theatre, and you can smoke, converse and relax within your own car without the least disturbance to your neighbors in the audience.

The size of drive-in theaters presented its own unique set of problems. One such problem needed to be resolved before the drive-in concept could be realized. Existing speakers tended to project sound that could be heard in all directions. A better sound system would direct the sound toward the movie viewers. The Photophone engineering department of the RCA Victor Company experimented with directional sound and finally succeeded in producing "controlled directional sound." Three of the new speakers were placed near the movie screen in front of the cars. Though not perfect they were considerably improved over existing technology. Still, occupants in cars at the rear of the theater couldn't hear the sound as well as those in the front. This breakthrough technology was incorporated into the Camden drive-in[68] and a version designed by Western Electric was employed in Milford's new drive-in theater.[69] In spite of the engineering efforts on drive-in acoustics, neighbors still complained about the loudness of the speakers. Although some drive-ins used individual speakers hanging inside each car from the outset, most of the early theaters converted to the less obtrusive listening devices starting in the late 1940s.[70]

The night before the grand opening of the Milford Drive-In Theatre, a special preview was held for town officials, state representatives and friends. On Friday night the general public was invited for the first time. The new drive-in could accommodate 500 cars on its terraced rows and it was filled to capacity. At eight o'clock the projector flickered and illuminated the largest movie screen in Connecticut, measuring 45 feet high and 55 feet across. Connecticut's first drive-in movie theater was open for business.

Seven nights a week, from 8:00 p.m. to 2:00 a.m., the new theater showed feature movies, short subjects, cartoons, and newsreels. The menu of shows changed twice weekly, on Wednesdays and Sundays. When it opened, the theater had a staff of 35 including ushers who rode bicycles as they escorted cars to their parking spots. The conveniences of this new type of theater were touted in the newspaper. "Occupants of each car will enjoy the privacy of their own car, smoking or talking among themselves without disturbing others. One may dress entirely to suit himself, a welcome feature during the warm Summer evenings."[71] Another advantage was there would be no need to hire a babysitter. "There'll be no need of hiring a maid to look after the children for you'll be able to bring them along and when they get sleepy, they can slumber perfectly in your own car until you return home."[72] "Patrons will enjoy all the advantages of a feature picture showing right in their own homes."[73] The theater also promised to show movies regardless of rain or fog.

Program from the Milford Drive-In Theatre, June 1939
Author's Collection

The popularity of drive-in theaters grew significantly after World War II. Shortly before the war there had been 160 such theaters around the United States. By 1949, there were more than a thousand countrywide[74] and by 1953 there were nearly 4,000 outdoor theaters.[75] Drive-in theaters continued emphasizing convenience[76] with one in California offering laundry service with washed and dried clothes ready to be picked up at the end of the feature movie. Another in South Carolina offered a grocery shopping service with groceries delivered to the car while its occupants enjoyed the film. In 1950, a drive-in in North Haven, Connecticut started offering church services on Sunday mornings during the summer months.

Many drive-ins offered additional entertainment activities for its customers. The rationale behind this was to encourage viewers to arrive early and eat at the concession stand. Over time, concession sales accounted for as much as sixty percent of a theater's revenue. With kids under age ten admitted free of charge, the theater owner more than made up for the free admission with the number of hotdogs and sodas the children consumed. In the 1950s, the Milford Drive-In hired a clown named Bozo Kelly, who billed himself as "King of the Clowns," and offered pony rides to enterain the kids before the show. In the 1960s the Milford theater provided free fire engine rides for the kids every night.

Over the years, forty-two drive-in theaters have dotted the state of Connecticut but now only a handful are still in operation. Drive-in theaters soared in popularity in the 1950s and 1960s, but by the 1970s they were facing financial problems. There are many reasons for the demise of the drive-in. First-run movies became expensive and difficult to obtain for a single theater. As indoor, multi-screen theaters increased in number they were better able to afford the up-front cost of the most recent films. Drive-ins resorted to second rate movies and "adult" flicks. With that sort of fare the attraction for a family to view a film from the comfort of their car diminished quickly. Increased choices of television programming, cable television, and movie channels eliminated the convenience factors that helped build the open-air movie industry. With revenues down and as land values increased, property taxes became prohibitively expensive for huge drive-in parking lots that were unfilled most nights.

In the northeast, the problems were compounded by the short viewing season. Most theaters were open nightly during the summer months and weekends in spring and autumn. During the winter months the theaters were closed altogether. To help offset falling revenues, the Milford Drive-In opened its doors on weekend days for the Keet's Flea Market that was established there in 1967. Milford Drive-In eventually closed and was torn down in February 1988 to make room for a new, indoor, multi-screen theater – Showcase Cinemas. That too has since closed.

When the projector at the Milford Drive-In showed its last credits, flickered briefly, and turned to black a little piece Americana died with it. In its heyday the theater provided an inexpensive, convenient and novel entertainment venue that appealed to families. Clowns, pony rides, fire engines, hotdogs, popcorn, soda and a movie on a giant screen. What's not to like?

Please....
DO NOT TURN ON YOUR LIGHTS WHEN LEAVING THEATRE
EXIT TO THE RIGHT!
Automobiles can enter and leave at any time To avoid undue disturbance, leave as quietly as possible. Incoming and outgoing cars will in no way interfere with either sound or vision. Last, but not least, - tell your friends about this unique theatre - and get the regular Drive - In habit yourself.
Rest rooms in center of Fourth Ramp.

Milford's Own Father Flanagan

When J. Edward Slavin of Milford decided he wanted to accomplish something important there was no stopping him. He had a vision for helping young people avoid following a life of crime. Slavin believed that if he could intervene early enough in the lives of at-risk boys and girls they would become good, law-biding citizens instead of law-breaking criminals who are an expense to society. Slavin once said, "Do you know that we in America have the largest jail and prison population in the world? That proves we didn't spend money in the right place. We spent it at the top, creating large police departments and other agencies for the prevention of crime and enforcement of law and order, while we neglected the bottom where crime starts."[77]

Logo Patented by Slavin
U.S. Design Patent
Issued June 6, 1939

Elected New Haven County's High Sheriff in 1934 Slavin, known as "Jack" to his friends, started a career that would span nearly forty years. One of the challenges facing Slavin was the large number of young people who had brushes with the law. During his first year in office he formulated a plan to divert them from going down the path toward a life of crime.

He put his plan into action and started the First Offender Club. Members of the club would receive a pledge card, badge and a monthly newsletter. For several years, Slavin produced a weekly radio program heard coast to coast on the Mutual radio network and he solicited members over the airwaves. Within a few years, more than 30,000 children took the pledge not to become a first offender or get a police record, and to cooperate with authority figures.

Sheriff Jack's First Offender Club Pledge

Sheriff Slavin had bigger plans than simply a radio club. He envisioned a village for boys where troubled youths could live, work, and learn as a way to redirect their energies away from a life of crime. He was inspired by the success of a town in Nebraska, founded by Father Edward J. Flanagan in 1917. By 1940, Father Flanagan's humble Home for Boys had grown into a fully functioning community known as Boys Town located about ten miles outside of Omaha. Flanagan believed there was no such thing as a bad boy and that troubled kids deserved a second chance. He was adamant about not putting boys in reformatories or prisons alongside hardened criminals; this would only result in the boys learning the trade from more experienced offenders. Intervention could be successful if the boy could be reached "before the antisocial pattern had become too strongly fixed."[78]

Flanagan's labors had won national acclaim and in 1938 Spencer Tracy and Mickey Rooney starred in a feature film about his efforts and successes. Tracy won the Academy Award for best actor for his portrayal of Father Flanagan, and later presented it to then Monsignor Flanagan and had it inscribed, "To Father Edward J. Flanagan whose human qualities and inspiring courage were strong enough to shine through my humble effort."[79]

Not looking to start his own plan with a humble effort, J. Edward Slavin considered purchasing Charles Island off the coast of Milford in 1938. The Dominican religious order had used the island as a retreat center since 1929.

Slavin negotiated with the Dominican Fathers to use their facility as a school/camp for his First Offender Crime Prevention Club. On the 19th of September 1938, the *New York Times* reported that Slavin had announced his intent to purchase Charles Island for his crime prevention effort. The purchase of the island was never consummated. It is probable that events two days later undermined the deal. On September 21st, the Great New England Hurricane of 1938 pummeled the Connecticut coast. With sustained winds of over 90 mph combined with 14-18 foot tides, the retreat buildings on the island suffered devastating damage. Slavin's bid to purchase the island was withdrawn. The storm damage, combined with concerns over the risks involved in ferrying boys back and forth over potentially dangerous waters, convinced him to look elsewhere.

Slavin considered other properties for his village including controversial acreage in Southbury. With Nazism on the rise in 1937, an organization known as the German-American Bund acquired property in Southbury for a camp for American youths of German descent. The organization claimed it would be a youth camp with no military influence though guards would wear uniforms bearing swastikas on their sleeves. An outcry from the townspeople resulted in strict zoning laws that prevented the group from completing their plans. In March 1939, Slavin negotiated with the Bund to acquire the property for his First Offender camp but the new regulations restricted use of the land to farming and residences. Slavin's planned use would have required zoning changes that might have allowed organizations like the Bund back into Southbury. Slavin continued to look elsewhere.

Jack Slavin found another property - Skyline Farm in Becket, Mass. - in June 1939 and leased it for a one year period for his First Offender Club camp.[80] It is uncertain whether his Becket camp ever got off the ground, but soon his sights again focused on Milford. Slavin's progressive plan was eventually implemented but not on Charles Island or in Southbury or Becket. In 1941, Sheriff Slavin and his associates acquired 77 acres, known as Daniels Farm, from Harry and Pearl Daniels. A few months later H. Sanford Osborne donated five more adjoining acres to their effort. In 1942, Slavin established *Boys' Village* in Milford.

The project was not without its critics. Neighbors to the property expressed concerns about bringing what they perceived as undesirable elements into their neighborhood and since some of the boys would be attending Milford schools they felt it would burden the taxpayers. Slavin defended his effort by pointing out that his facility would be "…neither a penal institution nor a reform school. The fair-minded citizens of Milford, where I have been a resident and voter for nearly a quarter of a century, I believe, have confidence enough in me and know me well enough to know that I would not bring anything to Milford that would not be an asset to that beautiful town."[81]

Boys' Village opened its doors in 1944. With a 14 room farmhouse, small cottage, dairy barn, and poultry buildings it was originally designed to accommodate sixteen boys from ten years of age. Patterned after a New England village, it offered communal living, educational and training facilities for industry and farming, and a psychological clinic. The boys grew most of the food they ate and were responsible for performing chores around the facility.

Early Days at Boys' Village
Courtesy of Boys & Girls Village

Slavin's often-stated goal was, "to provide a village of opportunity for the homeless boy, where he may develop a spirit of self respect, a love for work, and a desire to forge ahead through honest industry...I really believe all boys have good in them if they are shown the right way. I always believed that if you keep a boy busy he won't get into trouble. I'm not interested in how much it costs to grow a boy. I'm interested in what kind of boy he'll make."[82] He laid out the goals of Boys' Village, which were relatively simple in concept:

1. To establish and conduct a farm for boys on a plan sufficiently extensive to afford instructions.
2. To restore handicapped and homeless boys in need of care and protection to a normal life wherever possible through a carefully planned and executed manner, involving relief, employment, medical care and education.
3. To establish and conduct a place for the social betterment of young boys.
4. To establish, maintain and provide a place for young boys so as to give them an opportunity to grow and develop in "social usefulness."

The village was designed to operate differently than the more traditional homes for boys. An early brochure[83] described the experience:

> The one inflexible rule of Boys' Village is that its boys shall not be regimented. The atmosphere is personalized and homelike, and the boys are guided rather than compelled by a trained staff. The boys live normally and wholesomely, with personal interests, possessions and friends, and they attend the churches of their choice and the Milford public schools where many of them are at the head of their classes. A sense of responsibility and self-sufficiency is developed in them to a far greater extent than is possible in "institutionalized" homes.

Original Buildings at Boys' Village
Courtesy of Boys & Girls Village

J. Edward Slavin was a visionary who believed in reform but didn't believe the traditional reformatory system offered youths a chance.[84] Slavin even wrote a script for a film along these lines that was produced in 1939. The film was *First Offenders* and had the tagline, "Stop turning kids without a chance into men without hope!"[85] The movie received favorable reviews, one stating that it "deals intelligently and forcefully with the ever growing problem of delinquent youth."[86]

The film's plot involves a young district attorney (played by Walter Abel) who is dissatisfied with how juvenile delinquents are sent to prison where they are exposed to calloused criminals. He leaves his position, obtains the financial assistance and support from businessmen in his community, and opens a trade farm where troubled boys can learn work skills. He finds that treating the youths with kindness wins over even incorrigible youths, until a young man (Johnny Downs) with a grudge against the farm's founder arrives. He proves to be troublesome to the point there is danger the facility might close. Gradually he comes to understand what the former DA is trying to accomplish and he too is won over.

Scene from *First Offenders*
Author's Collection

MILFORD *Lost & Found*

Jack Slavin could be found in print media as well as radio and film. In 1945, he published several comic books under the banner *Courage Comics* and under the auspices of Boys' Village. A search of comic book references locates only three issues of *Courage Comics* - #1, #2, and #77 with the first issue being exceedingly scarce. The themes of the stories were courage in the face of adversity and included scenarios relating to crime, athletics, and heroism in World War II.

Characters included the likes of U. S. Navy Lieutenant Chick Courage, boxer K. O. Brown, cowboy Buck Dennis, ace reporter Dennis Dean, Scartoe the Coyote, and a Belgian Shepherd named Red Badge. One of the recurring characters in his stories closely resembled Slavin himself. With art reflecting life, "Sheriff Jack" would save young offenders from a jail sentence, preventing them from being exposed to hardened criminals, saving them from a life of crime by taking them under his wing, and having them join the First Offender Club.

Sheriff Jack
Courage Comics #77

Courage Comics #77
Author's Collection

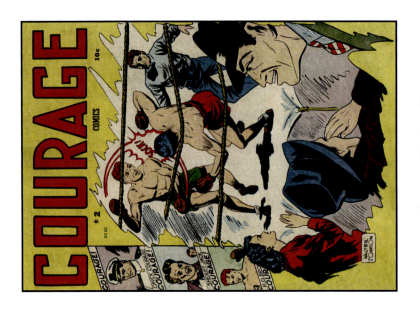

Courage Comics #2
Author's Collection

Going over Plans for Expansion of Boys' Village
(L to R – Architect Henry S. Kelly, Albie Booth, Daniel J. Adley, J. Edward Slavin)
Courtesy of Boys & Girls Village

J. Edward Slavin was the original president of Boys' Village and surrounded himself with people who could help fulfill his dream. "The board of directors of Boys Village is composed of practical men who have made a success in their individual fields."[87] None accepted compensation for their participation. Slavin selected William F. Hayes, former chief jailer for New Haven County, to be vice-president; Yale football legend Albert "Albie" Booth for treasurer; and home builder Peter Juliano as secretary. Members of the board included Stanley Komykowski, a prominent 4-H member who worked for the U.S. Department of Agriculture, as well as trucking company magnate and former New Haven Police Commissioner Daniel J. Adley.

J. Edward Slavin resigned his post as president of Boys' Village in 1947 and Daniel J. Adley was named to fill the position. Adley was a longtime friend of Slavin and supporter of his efforts. He and his four brothers and sisters were orphaned after their father was killed in a railway accident and their mother died giving birth a few months later. The children were placed in an orphanage and later Daniel was moved to Connecticut Junior Republic in Litchfield. In spite of their difficulties as children Daniel Adley and his brothers founded Adley Express, one of the largest trucking companies in the northeast. There could be no better man to guide Boys' Village than Adley who not only had financial savvy but also had first-hand experience in group home environments. He had a very personal and emotional motivation to see Slavin's vision fulfilled.

Slavin also stepped down as High Sheriff but certainly didn't retire. Instead, he implemented another plan to help support Boys' Village. His latest venture involved a traveling crime education center he called "Jail on Wheels." He outfitted a bus with exhibits displaying modern equipment and methods police used in outwitting criminals. Included in the traveling exhibit were descriptions of the science of fingerprints, recording devices, forensics techniques, a lie detector, and means of restraining and punishing criminals. The most memorable exhibits were an actual jail cell and an electric chair identical to the one used at the state prison in Wethersfield. Slavin's intent was to discourage young people from pursuing a life of crime by showing them the consequences of their wrongs.

He charged no admission fee and Jail on Wheels relied on donations from visitors to pay its expenses. After one year of traveling the country, more than a million people had toured the exhibit and Slavin paid off the remaining debts for Boys' Village. Immediately thereafter, Boys' Village started plans for expansion. The Village had been so successful that human services agencies from around Connecticut had made requests on behalf of another 150 boys.

Jail on Wheels Visiting Downtown Waterbury

Boys' Village is still operating today, re-named Boys & Girls Village, at its original site on Wheelers Farm Road. The facility has grown tremendously from its original plan. The number of boys and girls it serves has grown from a modest number during its first year of operation to over one thousand clients in 2008. Although relatively few of those served today live on-campus, residential facilities are still an important part of the culture at Boys & Girls Village. Abiding by the original plan envisioned by J. Edward Slavin, and continued by men like Daniel J. Adley, Boys & Girls Village continues to serve the community by being a village of opportunity for young people who need a helping hand.

Perhaps the efforts of Boys & Girls Village can best be summed up with its founder's own words. "I believe in giving an American kid a chance to grow right."[88]

Close Shaves for Milford

New England, Connecticut in particular, has been home to many of the prominent manufacturers of shaving products in the United States. The reasons date back to the technical skills cultivated here from the earliest industrial days when Eli Whitney developed a system for producing identical and interchangeable parts for use in musket production. In the years that followed, the machine tool industry flourished, especially in Connecticut. Tool making, metal stamping, turning, threading, shaping, lapping, cutting, milling and grinding were technologies that developed here and they fostered the growth of many related businesses. The enormous firearms industry in Connecticut – including Colt, Remington, Sharps, and Winchester – took full advantage of these technologies. Numerous other industries developed as a direct result of the expertise that was resident here and the skilled labor force that lived here.

At times there weren't enough skilled laborers available to fill the needs of the local industries. In August 1879, Bridgeport's Frary Cutlery Company brought 130 cutlers from England to work in their shop. The workers and their families arrived from Sheffield, one of the chief cutlery centers in Europe. The Frary Company paid their travel expenses and set them up in housing in East Bridgeport. This was just the start. The company's owner planned to bring an additional 500 English and German cutlers to Connecticut later that year.[89] The Frary Cutlery Company eventually became the largest cutlery company in the United States. With the machine tool and cutlery industries entrenched in Connecticut the stage was set for the eventual mass production of shaving products that would utilize those skill sets.

During the centuries before modern shaving systems were developed, knives (and later straight razors) were the weapons of choice to attack facial hair. The more modern design – the hoe-shaped razor - was developed in the 19th century and made use of blades that could be removed in order to be re-sharpened. It was in 1903 that regally-named King Camp Gillette invented double edge blades that were disposed of after several shaves instead of re-sharpening them. His system required the user to handle the blades in order to place them in the razor.

The potentially dangerous attribute of Gillette's double edge razor provided an opportunity for improvements by another inventor. The history of SCHICK® razors and blades dates back to the early twentieth century when Colonel Jacob Schick invented the first electric razor. Born in Ottumwa, Iowa, Schick joined the U.S. Army in 1898 and served in the Philippines. He was later transferred to Fort Gibbon, Alaska at the confluence of the Tanana and Yukon Rivers. Schick was a creative man who could take an idea and make a working model of it. For example, when in the army stationed in the Yukon he invented and built a shallow draft boat, known as the General Jacobs boat, that could carry fifty tons yet drew only one foot of water.

After he left the army in 1910 Schick decided to work in mining operations in British Columbia. It was during this period that he formulated his idea for a waterless, soapless shaving system; Schick was finding it difficult to shave in the 40° below zero temperatures. The opportunity to work on his invention came when he injured his ankle and was laid up for several months. His plans drawn during this time formed the basis for the electric shaver he would eventually market.

Jacob Schick had difficulty attracting the attention of companies to manufacture and market his novel product so he decided to form his own company. He had also invented two pencil sharpeners, Pencilaid and Pencilnife, and in order to finance his electric shaver operation he manufactured and marketed them with marginal success. Then, drawing on his experience in the army, he invented another significant advancement in shaving. Using a concept from the repeating rifle, he designed a razor that stored blades in the handle that could be loaded into shaving position without ever touching them. This was a huge improvement over Gillette's double edge blades that required the user to handle them in order to place them in the razor. Schick was hopeful this product would provide him the capital to finance the production of the electric razor he had invented years before.

Schick launched his novel Repeating Razor in 1926 and it became a huge success. He began production of the razor in Newark, New Jersey but in June 1926 he moved his factory to the Sound Beach section of Stamford. In spite of the favorable response to his Repeating Razor, Schick firmly believed the future of shaving was in the electric shaver market. In 1929, he formed a separate company and started to manufacture and sell his electric shaver. Within two years he built another plant in Stamford employing 100 people.

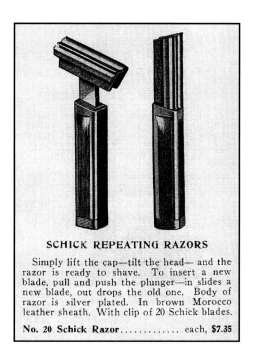

Jacob Schick's Repeating Razor
Smith Brothers Hardware Catalogue
Author's Collection

With all the success that followed the growth of the electric shaver business Colonel

Schick decided to take some legal but unpopular measures to protect his profits. In 1933, he established a corporation named Schick, Ltd. in the Bahama Islands. According to the *New York Times*, he "assigned his royalty income from the American operating company to the foreign corporation."[90] On December 19, 1935, with a special dispensation from the Prime Minister of Canada, Jacob Schick became a Canadian citizen. Friends of his claimed he had moved to Canada due to health reasons but others were more suspicious. Three days after becoming a Canadian citizen he formed three more corporations in the Bahamas – Schick Industries Ltd., Schick Shaver Ltd., and Schick International Ltd. He proceeded to transfer 57,000 shares of his American company, Schick Dry Shaver, Inc., into the new foreign corporations.

All this financial maneuvering caught the attention of the United States Congress and they held hearings in 1937 regarding loopholes that allowed the avoidance of taxes on corporate profits. They focused on seven individuals, including Jacob Schick, as glaring examples of how the tax laws could be legally avoided. Senator Patton Harrison of Mississippi spoke specifically about Colonel Schick:

> "It is very interesting to note at this time that Colonel Schick's change of citizenship was absolutely necessary for him to consummate this transaction and avoid taxes in the United States. There are laws designed to prevent American citizens from transferring American holdings abroad for tax evasion purposes. If an individual is neither a citizen of the United States nor a resident, there is no way in which our law as presently constituted can prevent him from transferring securities to whomever he pleases even though all the stock owned by this individual yield income through American companies."[91]

The flurry of inquiries into tax loopholes had no effect on Colonel Schick. This mechanically and financially inventive man was gravely ill at the time of the hearings and died a few weeks later. He was buried in his newly adopted homeland in Montreal's Mount Royal Cemetery.

So how did SCHICK® razors and blades end up being manufactured in Milford? Because Colonel Schick wanted to put all his efforts into his Schick Dry Shaver Company he sold his Magazine Repeating Razor Company to W. B. Lasher in 1929. Lasher was president of the American Chain & Cable Company in Bridgeport and he moved the manufacturing operations there from Stamford. During Lasher's ownership, the famous SCHICK® Injector razor, a direct descendant of the Repeating Razor, was introduced in 1934. Lasher's ownership continued until a manufacturer of pens acquired the company.

Writing instruments and shaving products had been intertwined from the early days. In 1945, Eversharp, Inc., a manufacturer of fountain pens and pencils, gained controlling interest in the Repeating Razor business. They renamed the shaving division the Schick Safety Razor Company and continued manufacturing in Bridgeport. Eversharp was still in the pen business ten years later and considered purchasing the Paper-Mate Pen Division of the Frawley Corporation. The deal fell through and Patrick J. Frawley sold his pen business to the Gillette Company. Eversharp, Inc. sold off its writing instrument business to the Parker Pen Company in 1957 and thereafter concentrated solely on razors and blades. A few months later Patrick J. Frawley was elected president of Eversharp, Inc.

Schick Safety Razor Facility, c. 1961
Jack Stock Studio, Derby, Connecticut

In 1959, Eversharp, Inc. purchased approximately forty acres of property off Route 1 in Milford for $256,000. There they built a large manufacturing plant, including research & development laboratories, designed by Caproni Associates of New Haven. The new facility, located off Home Acres Avenue, opened in 1961 and all operations were moved from Bridgeport to Milford.

Two years after Eversharp, Inc. opened its doors in Milford, another pen company acquired property for a large manufacturing plant a few miles away. In 1945, French entrepreneurs Baron Marcel L. Bich and Edouard Buffard started a small factory producing parts for fountain pens in Clichy, in the outskirts of Paris. Later, their operation produced ink refills for ballpoint pens, which were relatively new to the market. Ballpoint pens suffered from inconsistent performance and were expensive. Bich envisioned a pen that could be made inexpensively with improved quality. After several years of experimentation, Baron Bich introduced his improved ballpoint pen in 1953. Bich formed Société BIC and manufactured his new ballpoint pen, meeting with huge success in Europe.

BIC® Pen

Photo Courtesy of BIC Corporation

In 1958, Marcel Bich acquired controlling interest in the Waterman Pen Company, one of the oldest pen manufacturers in the United States. He named the new company the Waterman-BIC Pen Company. The Waterman Company had a factory in Seymour and the new company continued manufacturing operations there. This historic company, founded in 1884, was known for its high quality fountain pens, ballpoint pens, and pen & pencil gift sets with prices ranging from one dollar to eighty dollars. The primary focus of the new company shifted from more expensive pens to a new concept in writing instruments. Marcel Bich conceived the idea for a disposable ballpoint pen that would cost less than fifty cents. He designed a pen to be used until the ink ran out and then thrown away. The new pen had no moving parts and consisted of a metal ball-point at the end of a tube containing the reservoir of ink, and an outer, clear plastic tube. About three-quarters of the Seymour factory switched to producing this new type of pen.

The disposable pens sold well and larger production facilities were needed. In 1963, the Waterman-BIC Company acquired a Milford plant that previously housed the Norden Division of United Aircraft Corporation. By 1971, over 2 million inexpensive pens were being produced every day in Milford alone, in addition to the production at eighteen other factories around the world. The company became BIC Pen Corporation in 1971.

Baron Bich wasn't satisfied with producing pens and started to venture into other product areas. Bich had already shaken the foundation of one of Gillette Company's product lines. Gillette had produced PAPER MATE® pens since acquiring the business from Patrick Frawley and the business had suffered tremendously at the hands of the 19-cent BIC® pens. Another product in Gillette's arsenal was the Cricket butane cigarette lighter, a business it acquired in 1970. It was the leading disposable lighter at the time. In 1973, the Milford company again poked the bear named Gillette and began selling its own version of a disposable lighter with an adjustable flame. Within four years, the BIC® Lighter, with its unforgettable FLICK MY BIC® slogan, surpassed Cricket in sales. In 1984, Gillette stopped selling Cricket lighters, its business having been burned to a crisp by the upstart in Milford.

Not every product launched by BIC Pen Corporation was a success. In 1974 the company entered a totally different market – pantyhose. The company had hoped to capitalize on their reputation of value and their massive distribution network. The marketing and advertising staff decided to name their new product BIC® "Fannyhose." They test-marketed the product in Denver and Kansas City for a year and decided they needed to change the product's name to BIC® Pantyhose. Marketing vice-president John L. Paige told a reporter, "…many customers thought we were selling hose for women with big fannies."[92] The product was eventually taken off the market in the United States; it had proven to be too much of a stretch even for this usually successful company.

The BIC Company decided to poke the bear in Boston one more time. They introduced a shaving product – striking at the very heart of the Gillette Company's primary business. The audacious company first introduced its single-blade, disposable razor in Greece in 1974. Before long it was selling well in several countries in Western Europe, Australia, Japan and Canada.

As the introduction of the new shaver into the United States neared, the Milford plant was expanded to produce millions of razors. The BIC® Shaver was introduced here in 1976. The Gillette Company was on the defensive and that same year launched its twin-bladed GOOD NEWS!™ disposable razor. The Boston bruin was now angry and the war of disposable razors had begun. The Schick Razor Division of then owner Warner-Lambert Company waited on the sidelines to see if disposable razors would become a powerful force in the marketplace. They did; and a SCHICK® disposable razor pushed its way onto the battlefield in 1980.

With the machine tool and cutlery trades in southern Connecticut it was only natural that industries requiring these resources sprouted up nearby. Jacob Schick and Marcel Bich weren't the only shaving entrepreneurs to recognize the advantage of manufacturing their products here. At least two other electric razor companies took advantage of the resources this part of Connecticut had to offer. Lektro Shave Corporation produced electric shavers in Stamford and Remington-Rand (later Remington Products) manufactured them in Bridgeport.

For many years, once sleepy Milford was the front line in the battle for the morning shave, with two of the three combatants located within four miles of one another. The razor war continues to this day and it all started many years ago with the ambitions of a Baron, a Colonel, and a King.

References

Advance. University of Connecticut, September 1999.

Beers, F. W. *Atlas of New Haven County.* New York: F. W. Beers, 1868.

Biggs, Nick. "Tales from Merwin." *Columbia County History & Heritage*, Fall 2002.

Boys' Village: A Village of Opportunity for the Homeless Boy, Milford: Boys' Village, 1949.

Bridgeport Daily Farmer.

Bridgeport Post.

Bridgeport Telegram.

Burbank Daily Review.

Burton, Richard (editor). *Men of Progress: Biographical Sketches and Portraits of Leaders in Business and Professional Life in and of the State of Connecticut.* Boston: New England Magazine, 1897.

Collier, Edward A. *A History of Old Kinderhook.* New York: G. P. Putnam's Sons, 1914.

Colton, J. H. *Map of Connecticut.* New York: J. H. Colton's Geographical Publishing Establishment, 1854.

Courage Comics. Milford: J. Edward Slavin, 1945. No. 2 & 77.

Deming, Clarence. "Gunnery Sports" in *The Master of the Gunnery: A Memorial of Frederick William Gunn by his Pupils.* New York: The Gunn Memorial Association, 1887.

(Dooling, Michael C.) *The Art & Science of Shaving.* Warner-Lambert Company, 1994.

Downes, William Howe. "An Old Connecticut Town." *The New England Magazine*, November 1889.

Fairbanks, Lorenzo Sayles. *Genealogy of the Fairbanks Family in America 1633-1897.* Boston: Printed for the Author, 1897.

Hartford Courant.

History of Milford Connecticut 1639-1939. Federal Writers' Project, 1939.

Houghton, Walter H. et al. *American Etiquette and Rules of Politeness.* Chicago: Rand, McNally & Co., 1882.

Internet Movie Database – IMDB.com.

Irving, Washington. *The Legend of Sleepy Hollow.* New York: Harper & Brothers, 1897.

Koehm, Mary S. *Centum: A Legacy of Lamplight.* Milford: Academy of Our Lady of Mercy, 2005.

Korpalski, Adam. *The Gunnery 1850-1875, A Documentary History of Private Education in America.* The Gunnery, 1977.

Lambert, Edward R. *History of the Colony of New Haven.* New Haven: Hitchcock & Stafford, 1838.

Mathews, Mitford M. (editor). *A Dictionary of Americanisms on Historical Principles.* Chicago: University of Chicago Press, 1951.

Milford Associate Library, 1761. Manuscript in the collection of the Connecticut Historical Society.

Milford Town Record.

New Haven Evening Register.

New Haven Journal Courier.

New York Times.

Program for the Milford Drive-In Theatre. Milford, Connecticut, June 1939.

(Roy, Ralph Lord). *Church Directory.* Milford: Mary Taylor United Methodist Church, 1977.

Silverman, Sara. *The Nature of Camping.* Washington: The Gunnery, 2008.

Smith Brothers Hardware Company General Catalogue. Columbus: Smith Brothers, 1930.

Somers, Wayne (editor). *Encyclopedia of Union College History.* Schenectady: Union College Press, 2003.

Stray Shot. Washington, Connecticut: The Gunnery, March 1884, Volume I, No. 1.

The Dartmouth.

The Typhoon. Milford: Milford School Yearbook, 1922.

Ungdom paa Alveje. First Offenders movie brochure from its release in Denmark.

United States Federal Census, 1930.

Waterbury Republican.

Yale–Harvard Official Football Program, 1906.

Notes

[1] Lambert, *History of the Colony of New Haven*, 149.

[2] "Great Rally of the People!," *Hartford Daily Courant*, 27 February 1840, 2.

[3] Ibid.

[4] *Brattleboro Weekly Eagle*, 20 August 1849, 2.

[5] Old name for Seymour.

[6] According to Mitford M. Mathews (p. 954) the "land of steady habits" is Connecticut, alluding to the strict morals of its inhabitants.

[7] Region in southern Spain.

[8] Downes, "An Old Connecticut Town," 280.

[9] An Old English term for a person, more commonly used in describing a hapless person for whom nothing goes right.

[10] Irving, *The Legend of Sleepy Hollow*, 12.

[11] "One of Irving's Letters," *New York Times*, 9 August 1880, 2.

[12] "Ichabod Crane Once More," *New York Times*, 19 March 1898, BR 190.

[13] Silverman, *The Nature of Camping*, 2.

[14] *Stray Shot*, March 1917, 40.

[15] Deming, "Gunnery Sports," 98.

[16] *Stray Shot*, March 1917, 26.

[17] Korpalski, *The Gunnery 1850-1875*, 15.

[18] *Bridgeport Daily Farmer*, 16 August 1865, 2.

[19] *Stray Shot*, March 1884, 1. *Italics* in quote added for emphasis.

[20] "Campers to Revel in Milford Tonight," *Milford Citizen*, 17 July 1986, 1, 4.

[21] "Campers Enjoy Music, Games, Skits," *Milford Citizen*, 18 July 1986, 1, 4.

[22] "Yale Clinched with Harvard," *New Haven Evening Register*, 24 November 1906, 1.

[23] Ibid.

[24] Ibid.

[25] Milford Town Record, 26 October 1906, 220.

[26] "Autoists to Fight Milford," *New Haven Evening Register*, 26 November 1906, 1.

[27] "Milford Makes Big Auto Haul," *New Haven Evening Register*, 24 November 1906, 1.

[28] "Mrs. Herreshoff One of the Victims," *Hartford Courant*, 26 November 1906, 1.

[29] "Around Rhode Island," *Newport Daily News*, 24 November 1906, 4.

[30] "The Automobile Arrests," *New Haven Evening Register*, 27 November 1906, 6.

[31] "In Banker Taylor's Favor," *New York Times*, 27 December 1894, 14.

[32] "Family Skeleton Shown," *Boston Daily Globe*, 14 December 1900, 7.

[33] United States Federal Census, 1930.

[34] *Burbank Daily Review*, 9 February, 1953, 2.

[35] "Bayard Taylor in Court," *New Haven Evening Register*, 13 December 1900, 1.

[36] "Written on the Screen," *New York Times*, 17 September 1916, X7.

[37] "Written on the Screen," *New York Times*, 9 January 1916, p. X4.

[38] "Milford Beach is a Scene of 'Bloody Battle'," *Bridgeport Post*, 14 December 1915, 8.

[39] Ibid.

[40] *Cedar Rapids Republican*, 19 May 1916, 10.

[41] Ibid.

[42] Ibid.

[43] "Tie-Up Worst Since Blizzard of '88, Continues Most of Day," *New Haven Evening Register*, 14 December 1915, 1.

[44] "Written on the Screen," *New York Times*, 26 December 1915, 80.

[45] *The Typhoon*, 11.

[46] Somers, *Encyclopedia of Union College History*, 710.

[47] "Pigs, Pipers and Pajamas," *Advance*, University of Connecticut, 27 September 1999.

[48] *The Dartmouth*, 22 November 1907, 207.

[49] *The Dartmouth*, 9 November 1925, 3.

[50] "Bad Judgment," *Bridgeport Post*, 8 September 1920, 12.

[51] "Milford Student Shot by Cop; School to Sue Town," *Bridgeport Post*, 8 September 1920, 1.

[52] "Pupil Shot by Accident, Maher Says," *Bridgeport Post*, 9 September 1920, 2.

[53] "Milford," *New Haven Journal Courier*, 9 September 1920, 7.

[54] "Pupil Shot by Accident, Maher Says," *Bridgeport Post*, 9 September 1920, 1.

[55] "Milford's Bathing Discussion Extends to Other Shores," *New Haven Journal Courier*, 30 June 1921, 1.

[56] "One-Piece Bathing Suits for Women Barred at Coney," *Hartford Courant*, 8 May 1920, 1.

[57] "Atlantic City Bars One-Piece Bathing Suits," *Hartford Courant*, 25 July 1921, 1.

[58] "Milford's Bathing Discussion Extends to Other Shores," *New Haven Journal Courier*, 30 June 1921, 2.

[59] Ibid, 1.

[60] "Milford Bathers Must Wrap Up While on Street," *Bridgeport Telegram*, 24 June 1921, 32.

[61] "Milford Police Board Adopts Much Opposed 'Cover-Up' Ordinance, But Tells Chief to 'Use his Judgment'," *Bridgeport Telegram*, 9 July 1921, 1.

[62] "Milford Bathers Must Wrap Up While on Street," *Bridgeport Telegram*, 24 June 1921, 32.

[63] "Milford Bathers Scorn Proposed Cover-Up Rule," *Bridgeport Telegram*, 8 July 1921, 9.

[64] "Milford Police Board Adopts Much Opposed 'Cover-Up' Ordinance, But Tells Chief to 'Use his Judgment'," *Bridgeport Telegram*, 9 July 1921, 1.

[65] "Milford's Bathing Discussion Extends to Other Shores," *New Haven Journal Courier*, 30 June 1921, 2.

[66] "Opens Tonight!," *Waterbury Republican*, 26 May 1939, 26.

[67] R. M. Hollingshead, Jr., "Drive-In Theater," United States Patent # 1,909,537.

[68] "World's First Drive-In Theater Formally Opened," *Hartford Courant*, 16 July 1933, A4.

[69] "Drive-In Theatre Milford," *The Milford News*, 3 June 1939, 7.

[70] "Keeping Pace with the Drive-ins," *New York Times*, 25 May 1958, X5.

[71] "New Theatre on Turnpike Open Friday," *The Milford News*, 20 May 1939, 10.

[72] "Drive-in Theatre Milford," *The Milford News*, 27 May 1939, 9.

[73] "New Theatre on Turnpike Open Friday," *The Milford News*, 20 May 1939, 1.

[74] "Double Feature – Movies and Moonlight," *New York Times*, 1 October 1950, 182.

[75] "Keeping Pace with the Drive-ins," *New York Times*, 25 May 1958, X5.

[76] "Movie Novelty Develops into Big Business," *New York Times*, 4 September 1949, 47.

[77] "Boys Village is Sheriff's Dream Realized," *Waterbury Republican*, 23 July, 1944, 7.

[78] "Father Flanagan," *Hartford Courant*, 16 May 1948, A2.

[79] "Award to Mgr. Flanagan," *New York Times*, 1 March 1939, 26.

[80] "Mass. Farm Obtained for 'First Offenders'," *Hartford Courant*, 4 June 1939, C8.

[81] "Sheriff Slavin Assures Milford Farm For Boys Won't Injure Town," *Hartford Courant*, 2 January 1942, 9.

[82] "Boys Village is Sheriff's Dream Realized," *Waterbury Republican*, 23 July, 1944, 2, 7.

[83] *Boys' Village: A Village of Opportunity for the Homeless Boy*, Milford: Boys' Village, 1949, 3.

[84] "Sheriff Turns Island to Crime Prevention," *New York Times*, 19 September 1938, 21.

[85] Internet Movie Database, http://www.imdb.com/title/tt0031312.

[86] "First Offenders, Slavin's Story is at E. M. Lowe's," *Hartford Courant*, 25 March 1939, 8.

[87] "Boys Village is Sheriff's Dream Realized," *Waterbury Republican*, 23 July, 1944, 2.

[88] "Boys Village is Sheriff's Dream Realized," *Waterbury Republican*, 23 July, 1944, 7.

[89] "Workmen from Sheffield Coming Over to Make Knives in America," *New York Times*, 7 August 1879, 8.

[90] "7 Named as Using Devices to Reduce Big Income Taxes," *New York Times*, 19 June 1937, 5.

[91] Ibid.

[92] "We Didn't Mean That," *Hartford Courant*, 8 July 1975, 54.

CONNECTICUT HISTORY

Milford Lost & Found rediscovers events either lost in the dustbin of history or simply forgotten with the passage of generations and time. Some are historic, others just plain fun. All deserve to be remembered.

➢ Why were plays, novels, and romances banned from a Milford library?

➢ How did Milford receive the nickname "Sleepy Hollow"?

➢ What role did Welch's Point play in the history of camping?

➢ Why was the beach at Smith's Point once transformed into a desert, complete with camels?

➢ How did a constable cause a stir with fans before the Yale - Harvard football game in 1906?

➢ Why did boys from the Milford School parade downtown in their pajamas?

➢ Who was Laura of Lauralton Hall fame?

➢ When did Milford pass a modesty law requiring women to cover up on their way to and from the beach?

➢ What amusement sensation made its state debut here in 1939?

➢ Who founded the First Offender Club to help keep kids out of trouble?

➢ How did Milford become the front line in the battle over the morning shave?

$19.95

ISBN: 978-0-9627424-2-2